PIERS PLOWMAN

AND THE SCHEME OF SALVATION

AN INTERPRETATION OF
DOWEL, DOBET, AND DOBEST

BY ROBERT WORTH FRANK, JR.

ARCHON BOOKS   1969

821
65p
YF2

©Copyright, 1957, by Yale University Press
Reprinted 1969 with permission of Yale University Press
in an unaltered and unabridged edition

{Yale Studies in English, Vol. 136}

SBN: 208 00779 2
Library of Congress Catalog Card Number: 69-15683
Printed in the United States of America

TO
ROBERT WORTH FRANK
AND
MARTIN J. LOEB

Preface

THE scope and purpose of this study are explained in detail in the opening chapter. Stated in most general terms, the intention of the book is to provide a careful reading of a medieval poem, *Piers Plowman*. My aim has been to describe its form and explain its meaning. No more basic question, of course, can be asked about a work of literature. It was, however, the question that the poem evoked several years ago when I read it for the first time. I found it a work of tremendous power and enormous inventiveness, but I also found its form a puzzle and its meaning a mystery. The question demanded an answer, and I set out to find it if I could. The pages that follow contain my answer.

In its original form this interpretation of *Piers Plowman* was a dissertation submitted to the Faculty of the Yale Graduate School in candidacy for the degree of Doctor of Philosophy. It has subsequently been completely reorganized and rewritten for publication. The late Karl Young and the late Robert J. Menner supervised the original doctoral essay. To have had the counsel of two such eminent scholars was an inestimable privilege. Their kindness, their tolerance, and their wisdom were a lesson in the meaning of true scholarship. E. Talbot Donaldson and Morton W. Bloomfield encouraged me in this project when encouragement was most valuable, and I owe them a debt of gratitude. Benjamin C. Nangle, editor of the Yale Studies in English, has been very helpful with the problems of publication, and David Horne of the Yale University Press has given me the benefit of a most careful reading of my manuscript and of his expert editorial advice; I should like to thank them both.

The publication of this book has been made possible by a subsidy from the Committee on Publication of the Department of English of Yale University; I am most grateful to the Committee. Finally, I wish to thank my father-in-law, Dr. Martin J. Loeb, for his generous assistance with this study, only one example among many of his devotion to the scholarly life.

R.W.F., Jr.

Evanston, Illinois
July 1957

Contents

Cue Titles

NP-N	A Select Library of the Nicene and Post-Nicene Fathers of the Christian Church, ed. Philip Schaff, Ser. 1, New York, 1905.
OED	*A New English Dictionary on Historical Principles,* Oxford, Oxford University Press, 1888–1933.
Parallel Texts	William Langland, *The Vision of William Concerning Piers the Plowman in Three Parallel Texts, together with Richard the Redeless,* ed. W. W. Skeat, 2 vols. Oxford, 1886.
The Pardon	Nevill Coghill, *The Pardon of Piers Plowman,* Proceedings of the British Academy, *31,* London, 1945.
PL	J.-P Migne, Patrologiae Cursus Completus. . . . Series Latina, Paris, 1844–65.
Scriptural Tradition	D. W. Robertson, Jr., and Bernard F. Huppé, *Piers Plowman and Scriptural Tradition,* Princeton Studies in English, *31,* Princeton, Princeton University Press, 1951.
Select Wycliff	*Select English Works of John Wycliff,* ed. Thomas Arnold, 3 vols. Oxford, 1869–71.
Sermons	*Middle English Sermons,* ed. Woodburn O. Ross, EETS, o.s. *209,* London, 1940.
Speculum Christiani	*Speculum Christiani, A Middle English Religious Treatise of the Fourteenth Century,* ed. Gustaf Holmstedt, EETS, o.s. *182,* London, 1933.
Summa Theologica	St. Thomas Aquinas, *Summa Theologica,* translated by Fathers of the English Dominican Province, 22 vols., London, 1911–22; New York, 1922–1925. References are to part, question, and article, not to volume and page.
Vices and Virtues	*The Book of Vices and Virtues,* ed. W. Nelson Francis, EETS, o.s. *217,* London, 1942.
Yorkshire Writers	*Yorkshire Writers: Richard Rolle of Hampole . . . and His Followers,* ed. C. Horstmann, London, S. Sonnenschein and Co., 1895–96.

PERIODICALS

Anglia	*Anglia: Zeitschrift für englische Philologie*
ELH	*ELH: a Journal of English Literary History*
JEGP	*Journal of English and Germanic Philology*
MedAev	*Medium Aevum*
MLN	*Modern Language Notes*
MLR	*Modern Language Review*

PMLA	*Publications of the Modern Language Association of America*
RES	*Review of English Studies*
SP	*Studies in Philology*
Speculum	*Speculum: a Journal of Mediaeval Studies*
ZVgL	*Zeitschrift für vergleichende Litteraturgeschichte*

NOTE.   All quotations from *Piers Plowman* are from Skeat's *Parallel Texts* edition. References to the A or C version will be identified as A or C. When the version is not specified, the reference is to the B version.

I

Prologue

Piers Plowman enjoys a dubious distinction. Few will question its importance as a literary and social document in medieval English literature, but fewer still are certain of its meaning. Least understood is the second part: *Dowel, Dobet, and Dobest.* The purpose of the present study is to elucidate this portion of the poem. Since *Dowel, Dobet, and Dobest* constitutes two-thirds of the whole poem, to explain it will be to explain *Piers Plowman* itself in large part. Moreover, I shall provide some analysis of the first section, the *Visio,* and so sketch in the general scheme of the entire poem. I shall study the B-text version rather than the relatively neglected C-text, because the B-text, it is generally agreed, preceded the C-text, and because I believe one faces fewer problems working from an understanding of B to an understanding of C than one does working in the reverse order.

The interpretation is of two kinds: an explanation of the general plan and theme of *Dowel, Dobet, and Dobest,* and an analysis of lines, passages, and scenes—an *explication de texte.* My method of analysis is the use of relevant context. That is, I have tried to understand the literal text at any given point not only by examining it first in the light of the immediate context—the particular narrative situation or doctrinal discussion of which it is a part—but, when the immediate context did not sufficiently illuminate a passage, by turning to relevant material elsewhere in the poem—passages in which the same word is used, the same situation occurs, or the same idea is discussed. At times a still larger context is utilized—the historical context of current ideas and attitudes relevant to the passage under examination. I have tried always to be attentive on the one hand to the immediate context and to the whole poem and on the other to the historical context.

Lest there be some misunderstanding, I should add that I have not tried to place *Dowel, Dobet, and Dobest* in any particular doctrinal, religious, or political movement in the late fourteenth century. I believe this needs doing, but I also believe that some general understanding of the poem must come first. Once students have this to work with, they can hope to discover with some exactness the specific current of ideas in which the poem was moving. And when this has been determined, there will probably have to be a further refinement in the interpretation of the poem. Here I have used the *general* historical context—the ideas and doctrines current in the late medieval period; and I have used it for a *general* purpose : to illuminate key words, patterns of action, and doctrines in the poem.

My choice of historical materials has accordingly been eclectic. I have assumed that the poet of *Piers Plowman* was a man of some education, enough to utilize the more easily available sources of knowledge of his time. His method of quotation, however, suggests that his reading and education were largely catch-as-catch-can, rather than highly formalistic.[1] And so I have relied primarily on the common repositories of information and doctrine—the encyclopedias, the standard commentaries on the Bible, moral and religious poems and treatises, and sermons; I have avoided specialized materials, such as scholastic philosophy.[2] There is no intention to seek out the actual sources of the poem or its ideas.

My approach to the "allegory" of *Piers Plowman* should also be explained. The application of the term to the poem has served only to add to an already considerable confusion about the poem and its meaning. The word "allegory" is notably ambiguous. It is commonly applied to *Piers Plowman* because the poem employs personification, namely characters and significant details which are abstractions. A character is named "Thought" or a cart is labeled "Christendom." All that is allegorical about this, however, is the treatment of abstractions as though they were concrete—as though they were persons or things, for they are not really persons or things and we are not to take them as real. Only their names are literal; that is, the poet is really talking about *thought* and not a human being, and he is really talking about *Christendom* and not a cart, when he uses these names. And the statements of a personification—of the character "thought," for example—are to be read literally. There is no reason to suppose that there is a hidden, a second meaning in a speech by an abstraction. I shall attempt to explain why a character labeled "Conscience," say, appears at a particular point in the poem, and what is the significance of a character so named acting or speaking as he does. But I shall read the poem as a literal rather than an allegorical poem, and I shall be looking for literal rather than hidden, second, or "higher" meanings. In the few passages where the poet does intend a second meaning, this fact is quite independent of

---

1. Much the same view of the poet's learning is expressed by E. Talbot Donaldson, *Piers Plowman,* pp. 159–60. See also R. W. Chambers, *Mind,* p. 100.

2. I shall refer frequently to the *Summa Theologica* of St. Thomas Aquinas, but with no implication that the poet used it as a source or that he adhered to the Thomist philosophy. Because it surveys so many matters of doctrine and cites so many authorities, the *Summa* is a kind of dictionary of quotations and an encyclopedia of medieval moral and religious doctrine. I employ it in these functions.

the use of personifications. In these passages the poet makes it quite obvious that he intends a second meaning, and he usually explains his second meaning to us.[3]

One further word about the approach. I have exploited two formal elements peculiar to the work. One of these is its division into a number of dreams. Most medieval poets were content to frame their narrative within a single vision. There are ten in B,[4] including two dreams within dreams, a particularly striking innovation. The only reasonable explanation for this plurality of dreams, I believe, is that the poet used the individual visions as thematic units.[5] He developed a theme within a single vision, ended the vision when he had finished treating that theme, and began a new dream to develop a new topic. The two inner dreams serve the same purpose in special circumstances. When in the middle of a vision he must turn for a time to a different though related problem, he creates for his dreamer a dream within that dream; when finished with the interrupting theme, he returns the dreamer to the original vision. Therefore—in studying *Dowel,* for example—I shall look for the theme of the first vision, the theme of the dream within that vision and its relationship to the first vision, the theme of the second vision, and finally the theme of *Dowel* as a whole. I believe that we can understand the larger units, *Dowel, Dobet,* and *Dobest,* only after we determine the themes of the individual visions within these three. This explanation of the plurality of visions cannot be proved; but the several visions do exist and would seem to demand explanation. The supposition will be supported, however, if it works in practice: if each vision is shown to develop a central idea, and if approaching the poem in this fashion leads to greater understanding.

Another formal device in the poem is the interludes in the real world which precede the various dreams. Some of them are a mere four or five lines in length and seem intended only to drop the curtain for a moment in order that the audience may be made sharply aware one dream has ended and a new one is about to begin. Others, however, are developed scenes of forty lines or more, such as the exchange with the Minorite Friars (VIII.1–61) and the speech of Need (XX.1–49).

3. This matter is fully discussed by Leo Leonard Camp, "Studies in the Rationale of Medieval Allegory," unpublished diss., University of Washington, 1942. There is a summary of this important dissertation in *Abstracts of Theses and Faculty Bibliography, 1942–43,* Publications of the University of Washington, Theses Series, *8* (Seattle, 1944), 93–5. See also R. W. Frank, Jr., "The Art of Reading Medieval Personification-Allegory, *ELH, 20* (1953), 237–50.

4. R. W. Frank, Jr., "The Number of Visions in *Piers Plowman," MLN, 66* (1951), 309–12.

5. Cf. Gordon Hall Gerould, "The Structural Integrity of Piers Plowman B," *SP, 45* (1948), 61: "each new dream marks the beginning of a new stage in the long search for divine wisdom."

I believe that some of these interludes are introductions to the vision which follows. They motivate the dreams by grounding them in experiences in the real world. And at times they introduce or point up a theme developed in the vision proper. Medieval man believed that an intimate relationship existed between the real world and the world of dreams, that waking experience left its imprint on the dream life, and that the dream experience, properly read, could be a guide to action in broad daylight: in the dream world the future was foretold or problems in the real world were solved.[6] In much medieval dream literature the experience in the real world before the dreamer falls asleep explains or influences the kind of dream that befalls him.[7] These other works, however, do not, like *Piers Plowman*, employ a dramatic incident preceding the vision. Nevertheless, the interludes in *Piers Plowman* seem to be a development of this device in medieval dream literature and a reflection of the contemporary attitude toward dreams. I have looked for a relationship between each interlude and the dream which follows it. The validity of this assumption, as well as the other, rests on its successful application in reading the poem. It has helped me to see the main theme in several of the most difficult visions; perhaps it will help other readers.

The presence of these formal devices, I should point out, bespeaks for the poet of *Piers Plowman* a greater conscious artistry and sense of form than many critics have allowed him. And so does the general plan which I believe directed the development of the tripartite *Dowel, Dobet, and Dobest.* Thus, though a recent critic's reconstruction of the personality of the poet has many engaging insights, the present study would suggest a modification of his statement that "it seems improbable that any careful, detailed planning, any meticulously prepared and executed design played any part in the creation of this poem." [8] I, too, should hesitate to call the poet either careful or meticulous; there are many irrelevancies, many irregularities in the poem. But a plan and a concern

6. For the medieval attitude toward dreams see Walter Clyde Curry, *Chaucer and the Mediaeval Sciences* (New York, 1926), pp. 195–240, esp. 207–18. There is an interesting brief history and defense of medieval dream interpretation by a psychoanalyst in Erich Fromm, *The Forgotten Language: An Introduction to the Understanding of Dreams, Fairy Tales, and Myths* (New York, 1951), pp. 109–47, esp. 130–6. The poet's attitude toward dreams is expressed at vii.148–67.

7. Physicians recognized a type of dream affected by the waking experience, the *somnium animale.* See Curry, p. 207. Chaucer stated the doctrine in *The Parliament of Birds,* 99–105. This correlation between real world and dream world can be observed in varying degrees and in various forms in Chaucer's *The Parliament of Birds, The Book of the Duchess,* and *The Legend of Good Women* (cf. Curry, p. 238; also pp. 233–40); *The Pearl; Wynnere and Wastoure; Death and Liffe; The Testament of Love;* and, more obliquely, Gower's *Vox Clamantis* and *Confessio Amantis.*

8. George Kane, *Middle English Literature: A Critical Study of the Romances, the Religious Lyrics, "Piers Plowman,"* Methuen's Old English Library (London, Methuen, 1951), p. 243. For the complete discussion of *Piers Plowman* see pp. 182–248.

for organization are, I believe, apparent and do shape the poem, finally, into a unified whole.[9]

9. A good case can be made for William Langland as the name of the author of the poem. See R. W. Chambers, "Robert or William Langland?" *London Mediaeval Studies, 1,* Pt. III (1939, pub. 1948), 430–62; and E. St. John Brooks, "The *Piers Plowman* Manuscripts in Trinity College, Dublin," *The Library,* ser. 5, 6 (1951), 141–53. I myself believe William Langland wrote *Piers Plowman.* But since I am concerned in this study with the meaning, the organization, and the development of the poem, I have referred to the author of *Piers Plowman* as "the poet" in an effort to by-pass the controversial questions of multiple authorship and other nonliterary matters. For a discussion of the previous literature on these and other issues in the poem, see the indispensable article by Morton W. Bloomfield, "Present State of *Piers Plowman* Studies," *Speculum, 14* (1939), 215–32.

2

The Plan

A READER interested in the meaning of *Piers Plowman* has a variety of explanations to choose from, but one interpretation in particular, a composite work of several scholars, has achieved wide acceptance in Great Britain and the United States. The first expositor was Henry W. Wells. In a detailed analysis of the B-text, especially the second section, Wells argued that the definitions of the term "Dowel" describe the Active Life, and that this way of life is dramatized in the *Dowel* section. The definitions of Dobet describe the Contemplative Life, which is dramatized in the *Dobet* section. Dobest is the Mixed Life of both activity and contemplation, exemplified in the episcopal office, and the *Dobest* section treats of this way of life.[1]

Building on Wells' views, Nevill K. Coghill then suggested that Dowel is "the life of the manual worker and layman," Dobet is the life of the contemplative or clerk, and Dobest is the life of the bishop, who "cares for the salvation of men through the right administration of the instituted Christian Church." In addition, Coghill asserted that Piers himself is "the allegorical symbol" for these three ways of life, that his personal entries in the poem correspond to the divisions of the poem, and that the changes in his nature are relevant to those divisions.[2] Here and in his suggestion that *Dowel* contains the moral argument of the poem and *Dobest* the anagogical, Coghill was to some extent influenced by Howard Troyer's proposal that in treating Piers, critics should use the medieval method of fourfold scriptural exegesis and look for the literal, the allegorical or typological, the moral, and the anagogical meanings.[3]

Although Wells objected to what he called Coghill's "too literal view" and maintained that the "three states are psychological rather than sociological," saying "Langland's three lives are not vocational callings but mental states," he concluded that he and Coghill were es-

---

1. "Construction," 123–40. (When italicized, *Dowel, Dobet, and Dobest* is the title to the second part of the poem; when *Dowel, Dobet,* and *Dobest* are used separately and italicized, each refers to one of the divisions of the second part; when not italicized, they refer to the terms in the poet's text.)

2. *MedAev, 2,* 108–35.

3. "Who is Piers Plowman?" *PMLA, 47* (1932), 368–84.

sentially in agreement.[4] To these views of Coghill, together with Wells' modifications, the late R. W. Chambers added the authority of his approval, both by direct recommendation and by a long essay on the poem in which he followed and elaborated upon their analysis.[5] Since that time, most of the scholars who have discussed the meaning of *Piers Plowman* have accepted in greater or lesser degree the interpretation worked out by Wells, Coghill, and Chambers.[6]

Inasmuch as I must express throughout this study my disagreement with their interpretation, let me respectfully acknowledge at once the obviously valuable contributions these students have made to an understanding of the poem. We have all profited enormously by Wells' conviction that a plan and principle animate the work, by Coghill's many felicitous observations on the overtones of particular scenes and the meaning of specific passages, by Chambers' lucid exposition of the narrative. To argue against their general thesis is by no means to dismiss their work or deny its value.

Curiously enough, however, years before these men advanced the thesis, it was put forward and rejected by the German scholar Otto Mensendieck. Mensendieck is usually remembered only for his suggestion that *Dowel* is the poet's spiritual autobiography, a proposal which never met with acceptance.[7] Few recall what he had to say about the message of *Dowel, Dobet, and Dobest*. His analysis of this message does not depend entirely on the autobiographical thesis and deserves consideration on its own merits. *Dowel,* according to Mensendieck, recounts the poet's belief in early years in three ways of life, the Active, the Contemplative, and the Episcopal (Dowel, Dobet, and Dobest), a view the poet later rejected because he came to believe that there was only one way of life for all men: to be followers of Christ in poverty and love. *Dobet* does not preach a way of life better than that described in *Dowel;* rather it shows examples of life lived by the principles stated at the conclusion of *Dowel,* primarily the example of Christ. *Dobest* dramatizes the founding of the Church and the Christian community. Dobest is the perfection of good on earth according to the example of Christ's life (Dowel) and through the strength of Christ's work of salvation (Dobet).[8] What is particularly noteworthy here is Mensendieck's conclusion that the poet discards a belief in the Three Ways of Life and replaces it with a belief in one way of life for all; and that

4. "The Philosophy of Piers Plowman," *PMLA, 53* (1938), 339–49.

5. *Mind,* pp. 88–171. The commendation of Wells and Coghill is given on p. 102. See also his Warton lecture, *Poets and Their Critics: Langland and Milton,* Proceedings of the British Academy, *27* (London, 1941), 14.

6. A recent study influenced by this view is D. W. Robertson, Jr., and Bernard F. Huppé, *Piers Plowman and Scriptural Tradition.*

7. *Charakterentwickelung,* pp. 8–9, 15.

8. Ibid., pp. 53–6, 57 f., 60–1, 64.

the *Dobet* and *Dobest* sections show not different ways of life but the one way preached in the final passus of *Dowel*. Important, too, are his comments on the content of *Dowel, Dobet, and Dobest*. Mensendieck, I believe, came closer to revealing the meaning of the poem than anyone who has since written on it. My own interpretation, which has been worked out independently of Mensendieck's, is by no means identical with his, but it does proceed in the same direction. What he had to say about the poem deserves more attention than it has received, and I bring him forward as a fellow heretic who does not believe that *Piers Plowman* preaches the Three Ways of Life.[9]

There are a number of weaknesses in the theory of the Three Lives. One weakness is Coghill's appeal to the fourfold method of biblical interpretation.[1] There is not the slightest excuse for decking out a personification-allegory in the mystic garments of medieval scriptural exegesis. Personification-allegory, as I have observed already, is primarily literal and is not intended to carry more than two levels of meaning. The recent effort of Robertson and Huppé[2] to apply the fourfold method in detail is unconvincing. Fortunately, Coghill, although he invokes the method, does not really apply it.

A more critical weakness is Coghill's treatment of the titles. *Dowel*, he says, is not really concerned with Dowel as a way of life. *Dowel* contains the moral argument of the whole poem. The Life of Dowel has been presented in the *Visio*.[3] This imposes a most curious, halting plan on the work, for Dowel is exhibited first and then explained, but Dobet and Dobest are explained first and then exhibited. An embarrassment proceeding from the text seems to be responsible for this scheme: Coghill calls Dowel the Active Life, but there is much more

9. Several writers have expressed their disagreement with the theory of Wells, Coghill, and Chambers, but there has been no detailed counterargument. Gordon Hall Gerould expresses a demurrer in a footnote: *SP, 45* (1948), 75, n. 14. Howard Meroney provides a more vigorous objection in "The Life and Death of Longe Wille," *ELH, 17* (1950), 12–15. Meroney argues that the poem is concerned with the Purgative, Illuminative, and Unitive conditions of the soul, in the mystic tradition. These three conditions, he believes, are the Dowel, Dobet, and Dobest of the poem. The Purgative Stage comprises the *Visio, Dowel,* and *Dobet* as far as B.xv.189. The Illuminative Stage is contained in the remainder of *Dobet* and most of *Dobest,* i.e. xv.190–xx.212a. The Unitive Stage is given in the remainder of the poem. (Meroney, pp. 8–15.) Cf. also Donaldson, pp. 156–98, esp. 157–9, 169. Since this note was written, an extended critique both of Meroney's suggestion and of the doctrine of the Three Lives has appeared: S. S. Hussey, "Langland, Hilton, and the Three Lives," *RES, 7* (1956), 132–50. I regret that Mr. Hussey's excellent article appeared too late for me to make use of it in my text.

1. *MedAev, 2,* 109, 110, 114. See also Coghill's introduction to Henry W. Wells, *The Vision of Piers Plowman Newly Rendered into Modern English* (London, Sheed & Ward, 1938), p. xvii; and *The Pardon*, pp. 51–3.

2. *Scriptural Tradition, passim.*

3. *MedAev, 2,* 118, 125.

of the active life in the *Visio* than in *Dowel,* where the action is largely an intellectual and moral quest. Since, however, the poet gave the title *Dowel* not to the *Visio* but to the later section, the conviction must remain that he was really talking about Dowel in the *Dowel* passus.

There are several objections to the thesis that the Three Lives are the poet's Dowel, Dobet, and Dobest. For one thing, the poet was not well-informed about the doctrine of the Three Lives. He apparently did not know the term "Mixed Life" or any equivalent term, for he never used it, not even in the two passages where he came closest to describing the Three Lives; Thought's speech and Clergy's.[4] Nor does he use the terms "Active" and "Contemplative," which he knew, in Thought's speech. In Clergy's speech he uses the term "Active Life" with reference to Dowel, but does not apply the term "Contemplative Life" to Dobet, although Dobet seems to be the religious in part. The absence of the technical terms is puzzling if the doctrine of the Three Lives is of major importance.

Equally puzzling on this score is his treatment of the Tree of Charity scene, where Piers calls the three kinds of fruit on the tree marriage, widowhood, and virginity,[5] although it seems a golden opportunity to introduce the doctrine of the Three Lives. Stranger yet, in the C-text version of this scene the Dreamer is *puzzled* to see three kinds of fruit, saying he thought Jesus taught "bote two lyues," Active and Contemplative.[6] The passage suggests either that the poet did not know much about the Three Lives or that the doctrine did not much interest him.

His treatment of the Contemplative Life, again, is quite inadequate. In B he refers to the Active Life as the life of labor and the Contemplative Life as the life of prayer.[7] In C the Active Life is wedded life and the Contemplative Life is the life of chastity.[8] Chastity is one rule of the Contemplative Life, but only one. Of the Active Life the poet has

4. For Thought see VIII.78–97; for Clergy see A.XI.179–215.
5. XVI.68–72.
6. C.XIX.53–100. Henry Wells says this passage is "just such an ambiguous answer as a good teacher always gives when he knows that it is best for his pupil to find the answer in his own experience" ("Construction," 134). But there is no reason why a clear explanation of the Three Lives should be denied the Dreamer at this point. It is in statements made to the Dreamer much earlier in the poem, when, presumably, he was much less prepared for the full truth, that Wells finds a description of the Three Lives. Nor is there anything ambiguous about the answer. The division of those of good life into married folk, widows, and virgins was a commonplace. For example, *Vices and Virtues,* pp. 259–60, mentions this threefold division and refers to the parable of the sower. The threefold division apparently comes from the glosses on the parable (Matthew xiii:23). See *Catena Aurea, 2,* 494; Rabanus Maurus, PL, *107,* cols. 945–6; *Glossa Ordinaria,* PL, *114,* col. 131.
7. VI.249–54. Cf. the activities of Haukyn, the Active Man: XIII.224 ff.
8. C.XIX.71–80.

much to say, for he was profoundly concerned about the salvation of those in the Active Life, the great majority of Christendom—indeed, it is the problem to which the poem as a whole speaks—but that is another question. What the poet does and does not say about the Contemplative and the Mixed Lives, I conclude, does not encourage one to believe that they were matters of much concern to him.

Finally, it is important to understand the essential character of the Active Life and the Contemplative Life in the fourteenth century. The nature of both lives had been established by Gregory the Great:

> Activa enim vita est, panem esurienti tribuere, verbum sapientiae nescientem docere, errantem corrigere, ad humilitatis viam superbientem proximum revocare, infirmantis curam gerere, quae singulis quibusque expediant dispensare, et commissis nobis qualiter subsistere valeant providere. Contemplativa vero vita est charitatem quidem dei [et] proximi tota mente retinere, sed ab exteriore actione quiescere, soli desiderio conditoris inhaerere, ut nil jam agere libeat, sed, calcatis curis omnibus, ad videndam faciem sui Creatoris animus inardescat; ita ut jam noverit carnis corruptibilis pondus cum moerore portare, totisque desideriis appetere illis hymnidicis angelorum choris interesse, admisceri coelestibus civibus, de aeterna in conspectu Dei incorruptione gaudere.[9]

This description was easily known in the fourteenth century, for it was carried in the *Glossa Ordinaria*.[1] The two lives were similarly described in St. Thomas Aquinas' "Treatise on the Active and Contemplative Life" in the *Summa Theologica* (II–II, qq. 179–82), in Walter Hilton's *Epistle on Mixed Life*,[2] in the *Book of the Vices and Virtues*,[3] and in the *Meditationes Vitae Christi*, once attributed to St. Bonaventura. This last describes the Active Life as "that manere of lyuynge by the whiche a mannis besynesse stant principally in that exercise that longeth to his owne goostly profiȝt / that is to seie in amendynge of him selfe / as with drawynge fro vices and profitying in vertues; firste as to profite of hym self, and afterwardes as to his neiȝebore by werkes of riȝtwisnes and pitee / and dedes of mercye and charite." In the Active Life "a man trauaille and ȝeve hym to good exercise in prayere / and in studie of holy scriptures / and othere gode worchynges in comoun conuersacioun." The Contemplative Life is "restynge in contemplacioun / that is to saye in solitude at the leste of herte / forsakynge all worldes

---

9. Gregory discusses the two lives in *Moralium Libri Job*, vi, 37 (PL, *75*, cols. 760–6), and in *Homiliarum in Ezechielem Prophetam Libri Duo*, ii, 2 (PL, *76*, cols. 948–58), from which this passage is taken (col. 953).
1. PL, *114*, col. 287 (the gloss on Luke x: 38).
2. *Yorkshire Writers*, *1*, 264–92.
3. Pp. 220–1.

besynesse, with all his myȝte be about contynuelly to thenke on god and heuenly thinges / onely tentinge to plese god." [4]

It is therefore incorrect to think of the Active Life as a life of physical labor without any spiritual activity and to assume that a man in the Active Life could not be saved. Chambers seems to imply this when he says Piers realizes that following the Active Life of well doing "is not enough." [5] True, the Contemplative Life, according to the teaching of the time, was more meritorious than the Active Life; but the Active Life could suffice for salvation. It did not comprise merely the activities of the workaday world, as the words of Gregory and pseudo-Bonaventura prove. The poet equates the Active Life with bodily labor, as in the figure of Haukyn the Actyf Man, but the lessons Haukyn learns from Patience and Conscience prove the poet knew that spiritual concerns were consonant with the Active Life and were, indeed, an integral part of it if mankind was to be saved. As I have said, throughout the poem he wrestles with the question of how active, working men shall attain salvation. His answer does not rest on wholesale abandonment of the Active Life for the Contemplative; rather, as Konrad Burdach's researches have shown, it rests in part on the idealization of labor, embodied primarily in the figure of Piers the Plowman. [6]

As for the Contemplative Life, it does not consist of helping others, doing deeds of charity. Such actions are part of the Active Life, according to Gregory and the *Meditationes*. The Contemplative Life necessitated withdrawal from the world: its mode of life was to be quiet from all outward action; its goal was to see the face of God. The poet does not discuss these ideals, nor does he work them into the action of the poem. The narrative of Christ's life in *Dobet* is not a dramatization of the ideals of the Contemplative Life. *Dobet* concentrates on Christ's teaching of the doctrine of the Trinity, His example of charity to mankind by His sacrifice on the cross, and His release of man's soul from the devil by harrowing hell. This is action, not contemplation. Medieval writers on the Two or the Three Lives said Christ demonstrated the Contemplative Life, not in these activities, but in withdrawing to the hills to pray all night. [7] This is never mentioned in *Dobet*.

These are the basic weaknesses I see in the interpretation of Wells, Coghill, and Chambers. While I agree that the problem of salvation is the central issue of the poem, my own interpretation differs sharply

4. *The Mirrour of the Blessed Lyf of Jesu Christ: A Translation of the Latin Work Entitled "Meditationes Vitae Christi" Attributed to Cardinal Bonaventura, Made before the Year 1410 by Nicholas Love, Prior to the Carthusian Monastery of Mount Grace*, ed. Lawrence F. Powell (Oxford, Oxford University Press, 1908), p. 159.
5. *Mind*, p. 121.
6. See below, p. 14.
7. Cf. Walter Hilton, "Epistle on the Mixed Life," in *Yorkshire Writers*, I, 269. Also Gregory the Great, *Moralium Libri Job*, VI, 37 (PL, 75, cols. 760-1).

from theirs. I read the poem as a reply to the question which the Dreamer asks Holy Church in the first vision: How is man's soul lost, and how is it saved? The answer is divided into two main parts: the *Visio* is one, and *Dowel, Dobet, and Dobest* is the other. The two visions of the *Visio* present in narrative form the two antithetical principles which determine, according to the poet's view, whether man's soul will be damned or saved. The evil principle which leads to damnation is the way of Falseness or Wrong: it is the life governed by Lady Meed, the uncharitable, selfish desire for reward, especially money reward. The good principle which leads to salvation is the way of Truth: it is the life governed by the law of love. (This is stated explicitly by Holy Church in the first vision but is only implied by the action of the second vision, where the poet is dramatizing the way of Truth. He is saving more direct statement for *Dowel, Dobet, and Dobest,* in which the law of love is his unifying theme.) The good life is, in part, obedience to one's feudal duties (which he portrays later as ordained by the Holy Ghost and governed by the principle of love) and obedience to the command to do well rather than reliance on pardons and indulgences purchased with silver.

In asserting at the conclusion of the *Visio* that doing well was the way to salvation, however, the poet had answered one question but raised another: What must man do in order to "do well"? And implicit in this is an even larger question: *can* man do well? Or perhaps it can be phrased more exactly and positively: how is it possible that weak, sinful man can do well? In *Dowel, Dobet, and Dobest* the narrative raises these issues and resolves them. Holy Church had already answered the first question: what must man do if he would "do well"?— but in *Dowel, Dobet, and Dobest* the answer is repeated many times and in a variety of forms. It is to obey the law of love. In analyzing the three terms "Dowel," "Dobet," and "Dobest" in the *Dowel* section I have concluded that they do not possess individual meanings but are divisions of the generic term "Dowel" and that when using them the poet had always a single, all-inclusive concept in mind, not three separate concepts or ways of life.[8] My analysis of the *Dowel, Dobet, and Dobest* sections has led me to a similar conclusion: they do not show separate laws or ways of life. They show only how man has been enabled to obey the law of love to a greater and greater degree.

Implicit in the first question is a yet more disquieting query: *can* man do well? Can man obey the law of love, as he must do to be saved? The answer is that man can. The poet recognizes the dangers and difficulties; these provide the drama of his narrative. But he believes it is possible for man to do well and be saved. His positive faith rests

8. See Chap. 4, below.

on two insights. One is his belief that the Godhead in its Trinitarian aspect has by a series of acts enabled man to do well and so has made his salvation possible. The other is the belief that there is in human nature an inherent goodness, a semidivine quality, that implies man can do good and be saved. The first belief underlies *Dowel, Dobet, and Dobest;* it supplies the basic organization of the second section and is demonstrated there in detail. The second belief is assumed rather than demonstrated and pervades the entire poem. It is embodied in the figure of Piers the Plowman.

My own concern is primarily with the first belief; on the second I am content to follow Konrad Burdach's work on the figure of Piers. What he has to say about Piers, however, harmonizes so well with my own views about *Dowel, Dobet, and Dobest* that I shall summarize his conclusions and adopt them in my analysis.

The significance of Piers in the second part of the work is far from clear. In the first part, the *Visio,* he is a symbol of the good man who performs his feudal duties faithfully and follows Truth rather than Lady Meed. But after the *Visio* the references to him are obscure, and some of them appear to suggest that Piers is divine rather than human. For example, Clergy tells Conscience that Piers has said the law of love is the only knowledge of any value.[9] Soul says Piers alone sees into man's heart, quoting "Et vidit deus cogitaciones eorum" (probably Matthew ix: 4 and Luke xi: 17) and "Petrus, id est, Christus." [1] Piers explains the Trinity to the Dreamer and uses it to protect men's souls from evil.[2] Christ jousts with the fiend in Piers' armor, *humana natura.*[3] Christ gives Piers power to absolve men of their sins.[4] Grace makes Piers His reeve on earth.[5] In the conclusion, Conscience sets out, after the triumph of sin, to seek Piers Plowman, who can rescue mankind.[6]

There have been several attempts to wrest light from this darkness. Skeat explained Piers as a good man in the *Visio,* Christ in the latter part of *Dowel, Dobet, and Dobest.*[7] To Howard Troyer he is a symbol with multiple meaning, but always he symbolizes man.[8] Coghill analyzed Piers as a symbol for each of the Three Ways of Life.[9a] H. H. Glunz suggested he was first a godly king regulating the worldly concerns of

---

9. XIII.123-9.
1. XV.190-4, 203-6.
2. XVI.21-89. In C, Piers is replaced by Liberum Arbitrium (C.XIX.1-117, 138). This suggests that Piers is human, not divine.
3. XVIII.10-33. Also XIX.6-14.
4. XIX.177-85.
5. XIX.195-8, 208-9, 253-330; cf. 383-5, XX.318-19.
6. XX.380-3.
7. *Parallel Texts, 2,* xxv-xxvii.
8. "Who is Piers Plowman?" *PMLA, 47,* 368-84, esp. 370-3.
9a. *MedAev, 2,* 108-35. See also *The Pardon,* pp. 53-5.

his people in the *Visio,* then Christ before the Crucifixion, the Christ of the Crucifixion and the Harrowing of Hell, and finally the just God whose return on Judgment Day is awaited.[1]

These explanations assume that Piers was the poet's own creation. But what if Piers was not a completely original figure? The poem itself does not explain him clearly. It treats Piers as though he needs no explaining. Perhaps he existed in some context outside the poem that made him more easily intelligible to fourteenth-century readers than he is today. And why did Piers give the poem its title? He appears infrequently in the action and, except for the second vision, rarely plays a leading role. But if the figure of Piers were, in some form, popular and important in his own right, there would be more reason for him to give the poem its name.

Although there are no references to Piers outside the poem that cannot be explained as derivative from it, Konrad Burdach has shown that certain popular ideas current in the fourteenth century could have been, without too much difficulty, suggested by a character named Piers the Plowman. His contention is that the figure of Piers embodies these ideas. The name "Piers," a form of Peter, was one of the commonest of names, and so could stand for Everyman. It also suggested the Apostle Peter, the mightiest servant of Christ.[2] The name and role of plowman are even more significant. Because of its idealization in various passages in the Old and New Testament, particularly Ecclesiasticus vi: 18–19 and II Timothy ii: 6, and especially in Augustine, the plowman had become a symbol of human labor and primitive, uncorrupted human nature.[3] A strain of mystical thought conceived of human nature as having originally possessed both a human and a divine character. These speculations found this double nature in Adam. He was both the antithesis of Christ and like Christ.[4] It is this belief in a divine or semidivine element in human nature that the tradition emphasizes. The semidivine element is revealed also in such figures as Moses, Jacob, Solomon, and Peter.[5] Piers, Burdach believes, is created as an embodiment of this mysterious, half-divine essence in human nature.[6] He is, however, always human, never divine. The concept of Piers is rooted in the poetical and religious idea that the original pure nature of man stands in close affinity with God, whose image he is, and that his nature is manifested most completely in active work, faithful trust in God, simple love. He is the confession of man's closeness to God and of pure, loving humanity, and grows out of the conviction that this

1. *Literarästhetik,* pp. 534–5.
2. *Ackermann,* pp. 358–9.
3. Ibid., pp. 282, 294, 297, 341.
4. Ibid., p. 321; cf. pp. 315–19.
5. Ibid., p. 344.
6. Ibid., pp. 341–2.

pure humanity of labor and love in itself possesses the right to eternal life.[7]

The figure of Piers, then, reveals the poet's belief that man can be saved because of, as well as in spite of, his human nature. Piers symbolizes the suprahuman or divine element in human nature, which is proof that man is savable. Because of this divine element, man can do well (Piers in the *Visio*) and know and obey the law of love;[8] he can use the Trinity to ward off evil and lead the good life.[9] Man's nearness to divinity is proved by the union of human nature with the divine in Christ[1] and by God's entrusting to mankind the power of forgiveness of sins and the administration of the gift of grace.[2] Individual men of the Church may abuse this trust, but the semidivine element in human nature is proof that good men can be found who will administer these gifts properly. The search for Piers Plowman with which the poem closes expresses both the poet's sense that the Church needs reforming and his conviction that there can be found in humankind someone to do this work of reform. A good pope would be one possibility. But what is important is that this rescuer will be human in nature, a man rather than God.

Side by side, then, with the many views of man's wickedness in the poem is the assertion, through the figure of Piers, that there is in human nature a power of goodness which enables man to do what he must do to be saved. The poem is called the "Vision of Piers Plowman," therefore, because it gives us the poet's vision of man's capacity for salvation.

The poet, however, did not believe man would be saved solely because of his nature. Not only would this have been heresy, it would have been contrary to the poet's temperament. Such optimism about mankind was not for him. He had too keen an eye for man's darker nature. He believed he lived in an evil world among evil men, and he described this evil in almost loving detail. At the same time he clung to the belief that goodness, and consequently salvation, was possible. The tradition of the "divinity" of human nature helped keep him, one might say, from the sin of despair. Piers emerges in the poem when the way seems darkest.

The poet's hope that man can be saved does not rest exclusively, however, on any belief in the eternal goodness of his fellow men. What he devotes the body of his poem to showing is that man can achieve salvation because he is assisted by God. A divine plan, a scheme of

7. Ibid., pp. 351–3.
8. XIII.123 ff.
9. XVI.17 ff. Cf. *Ackermann*, p. 312.
1. XVIII.10 ff.
2. XIX–XX.

salvation, exists for man. The "goodness" of human nature is a mystical hope, embodied in the fleeting figure of Piers Plowman. The divine plan is a more rational belief, more orthodox and more readily demonstrable. It shows God's love for man, and the poet's account of this plan is designed both to instruct man specifically in what he must do to be saved and also to evoke, in response to the evidence of God's love for man inherent in the plan, a corresponding love of man for God.

In this divine plan each person of the Trinity has made His specific contribution to man's salvation. It is this which gives the second part its threefold division into *Dowel, Dobet,* and *Dobest.* One of the most attractive features of the theory proposed by Wells was the fact that the Three Lives provided ready-made a threefold pattern to explain the tripartite division of the second part. But the Trinity is such another ready-made threefold pattern and was, of course, known to every member of medieval Christendom, as the doctrine of the Three Lives was not.

Every reader of *Dowel, Dobet, and Dobest* has probably observed that one Person of the Trinity figures in each of the three divisions: God the Father in *Dowel,* Christ in *Dobet,* and the Holy Ghost in *Dobest.* Wells called it "a further organizing factor" in the poem. This use of the Trinity means, Wells suggested, that the poet believed there was a spiritual trinity in man.[3] But Wells never explained why the "state of mind" called Dowel should be associated with God the Father or why Dobet and Dobest are associated with the Son and Holy Ghost.

Rather than being "another organizing factor," the Trinity is, I believe, *the* organizing principle in the second part. It governs the order of events in this part, the theme of each of the three smaller divisions, and the use of the terms Dowel, Dobet, and Dobest as subtitles. We need not become involved in the doctrinal complexities of the Trinity; the poet uses it in a fairly simple fashion. Each Person of the Trinity is associated with a particular period of human history: the Father with the creation of the world and man; the Son with the events of Christ's life and death; and the Holy Ghost with the period after the Ascension. A kind of chronological order is achieved by making the Father dominant in *Dowel,* the Son in *Dobet,* and the Holy Ghost in *Dobest.* Moreover, the poet sees mankind assisted toward salvation by each Person of the Trinity. This gives a logical order to *Dowel, Dobet, and Dobest.* God the Father, in creating man, gave him an intellectual soul. It is by virtue of this intellectual soul that man is said to be created in God's image. It enables him to distinguish between good and evil and cleave to the good. This is the theme of *Dowel:* man's moral power, through God's gift of a rational soul, to know and obey the law of love,

3. "Construction," pp. 135–6. Cf. also "Philosophy," *PMLA, 53,* 348–9.

i.e. do well. God the Son released man from the bondage of hell, which was a consequence of Adam's sin. Moreover, this act, His Crucifixion, and His many acts of charity on earth gave mankind the supreme example of charity, to aid him in obeying the law of love. Christ also taught man the doctrine of the Trinity, which man had to know to be saved. And as the doctrine of the Trinity is explained in the poem, it becomes another counsel to obey the law of love. Through God the Son, therefore, man is better able to know and obey the law of love, i.e. do better. This is the theme of *Dobet*. The Holy Ghost gives man the final gifts essential for salvation: grace, the various vocations in this world, the evangelists and the four great Church fathers, the four cardinal virtues, the Holy Church, contrition and confession, and the priesthood. These, together with the power of forgiveness of sins granted mankind by Christ after the resurrection, enable man to obey the law of love most completely, i.e. do best. The giving of these gifts and man's use and abuse of them is the theme of *Dobest*.[4]

4. I shall not attempt in this study to answer the question of the possible influence of Joachimite ideas on the poem. But the plan which I have described for the poem, in which each Person of the Trinity plays in turn a part; the division of human history into three periods, each associated with one Person of the Trinity—a division clearly evident in *Dobet* and *Dobest* though obscure in *Dowel;* and the idea of progress implicit in this scheme and explicit in the titles *Dowel, Dobet,* and *Dobest*—these are concepts which might have their source in doctrines connected more or less remotely with the teaching of Joachim of Flora. They are, of course, older than Joachim. George Boas traces the Christian theory of progress as far back as a passage in Tertullian's *De velandis virginibus: Essays on Primitivism and Related Ideas in the Middle Ages* (Baltimore, 1948), p. 206. The doctrine of the three dispensations, one of the Father, one of the Son, and one (the present) of the Holy Spirit, was also part of the Montanist heresy. The doctrine of the three ages never died out. The most important revival of it occurred in the work of John Scotus Erigena in the ninth century: Boas, p. 202. The doctrine was given new impetus by Joachim of Flora in the latter half of the twelfth century. Joachim taught that there were three ages, each presided over by one Person of the Trinity. The first, the age of the Father, ended with Zacharias. The age of the Son began with Elijah, attained clarity with Zacharias, and was ending in Joachim's day. The age of the Spirit began with St. Benedict; it would last until the end of the world. The age of God the Father was described as the age of slavery, of babes, of carnal life, and especially of the married, the *ordo conjugatorum,* an image of the Father in His fatherly relation. This age was ruled by the attributes of the Father: power, dread, faithfulness. It was an age, therefore, of fear, law, and a life of labor. It was the age of laymen, and the special business of laymen is to work. The age of God the Son was the mixed life, between the flesh and the spirit. It was the age of the young, and especially of clerics, the *ordo clericorum,* an image of God and the Wisdom of God, for it is the business of the clerical order to speak and teach. Clerics live under the law of Christ. The age of God the Holy Spirit is the age of spiritual life. It has a peculiar *donum Spiritus Sancti* which is especially a *donum contemplationis.* In this age there will be an *ordo contemplantium,* and the whole Church will be an *ecclesia contemplativa.* The age will be ruled by the attributes of the Spirit: love, liberty, and joy. It will be an age of the old. Specifically, it will be the age of monks, the *ordo monachorum,* which is an image of the Holy Spirit, Who is Love, for those who despise the world are inflamed with the love of God and led by the Spirit, as the Lord was when He was driven into the desert. The monks represent all who live in ardent love under the Spirit. This doctrine of the three ages and the belief in a

This does not mean that the poem was written to expound this scheme. What the poet focuses on is man and the drama of his salvation. The divine plan is in the background. It gives shape and organization to *Dowel, Dobet, and Dobest* and animates the fundamental conviction pervading the poem that salvation is possible for man. At moments this or that aspect of the divine plan may become the center of attention, as in the crucifixion scene or the scene in which the Holy Ghost distributes grace to mankind. But the poet is looking at man rather than at the Triune God; it is the implications of the divine plan for human salvation that give the poem its direction; and it is the spectacle of man now blundering and now moving forward within the framework of this plan that gives the poem its drama.

------

coming reign of love, varying from sect to sect in details, continued in the thirteenth and fourteenth centuries. There are obvious differences between the content of *Piers Plowman* and the Joachimite doctrines, and yet there are haunting though obscure harmonies. The clearest parallels are the idea of three ages of the Trinity and the idea of progress which this implies. The organization of *Dowel, Dobet,* and *Dobest* may very well be a distant echo of Joachim's teachings. Cf. Henry Wells' brief comment on the similarity between the historical scheme of the poem and the historical teachings of Joachim: "Philosophy," *PMLA, 53,* 349. (The account of Joachim's teachings given above is based primarily on Henry Bett, *Joachim of Flora* (London, 1931), pp. 44–7. See also J. A. MacCulloch, *Medieval Faith and Fable* (Boston, n.d.), pp. 292–9; and Boas, pp. 209–15.

3

The Visio *and the Pardon Scene*

A GLANCE at the first part of the poem, the *Visio,* must precede any detailed examination of *Dowel, Dobet, and Dobest.* There is no need for minute analysis. The possible allusions to contemporary incidents and persons and the political ideas expounded there are not relevant to my purpose. But the reader does need to know the principal themes of the *Visio* and the relationship between this first section of the poem and the later visions before he can understand *Dowel, Dobet, and Dobest.* And since the Pardon Scene is the gateway to *Dowel, Dobet, and Dobest,* and several interpretations begin here, an understanding of this difficult scene is essential.

The two visions of the first part quite obviously form an artistic whole. Their title, the *Visio,* is evidence of this unity. They have, also, unity of place and time. The Dreamer falls asleep in the Malvern Hills at the beginning of the first vision and awakens there, "meatless and moneyless," when the second vision has ended.[1] We hear no more of the Malvern Hills in the poem. Moreover the field of folk is the scene on which the curtain rises for both visions;[2] we never see the field again. The action of these two visions takes place within a single day. The Dreamer falls asleep on a May morning, with the sun in the east, wakens for a moment, dreams again, and wakens from the second dream in the late afternoon, with the sun setting "in the south."[3] These unities bind the two visions.

This artistic unity is the reflection of a thematic unity. It is a view of man and his world that we have in the *Visio.* Its theme is man working in this world toward an eternal punishment or reward. The two visions are a dramatization of the way to damnation and the way to salvation. The theme is introduced figuratively in the field of folk and explicitly in the speech of Holy Church. The field of folk midway between the tower and the dungeon are the people of this world, Holy

1. A.Pr.5, VIII.130; B.Pr.5, VII.141; C.I.6, x.295.
2. A.Pr.17, 1.2, V.10; B.Pr.17, 1.2, V.10; C.I.19, II.2, VI.111.
3. This is the time scheme in A and B: cf. A.Pr.5, 13, v.5–8, VIII.129; B.Pr.5, 13, v.5–8, VII.140. The unity of time is destroyed in C by the long interlude between the first and second visions: C.VI.1–108. But as in A and B the Dreamer falls asleep for the first vision in the morning (C.I.6, 14) and awakens after the Pardon Scene in the late afternoon (C.x.294).

Church explains, their lives bounded by good and evil. The way to salvation is to follow Truth—that is, to love God and man. The way to damnation is to follow Wrong or False; specifically, to follow Lady Meed, to love worldly reward above all else.[4] The poet is stating the basic Christian doctrine: "These two loves, Charity and cupidity, are the two poles of the medieval Christian scale of values." [5]

Meed is for the poet the most evil and specific form which cupidity assumes in this world. Throughout Holy Church's speech, which is a guide to the doctrinal content of the *Visio*, Truth (the law of love) and money are the polar elements. Money belongs to Caesar; it is not God's. The polarity is most evident in the play on the word "treasure." Treasure is money, meed, worldly reward, but treasure is also the greatest good, truth.[6] In the narrative of Lady Meed, the poet dramatizes this pernicious and pervasive desire for worldly reward. There is an obvious contrast between the two ladies the Dreamer meets: Holy Church, the purveyor of right doctrine, "A loueli ladi of lere in lynnen yclothed," and Lady Meed, the seductress of mankind, clothed in a rich scarlet robe lined with fur and covered with gems.[7] Holy Church warns the Dreamer against Lady Meed and tells him charity and meed are antithetical and inimical principles:

> And what man be merciful · and lelly me loue,
> Schal be my lorde and I his leef · in the heiȝe heuene.
> And what man taketh Mede · myne hed dar I legge,
> That he shal lese for hir loue · a lappe of *caritatis*.[8]

The specific charge against Lady Meed is that she corrupts law in this world, and a good part of the narrative develops this charge. Many of the characters and personifications introduced belong to the machinery of law;[9] judges are bribed;[1] Peace, who has a complaint against Wrong, is bought off with a present "al of pure golde";[2] and the narrative ends with a judgment handed down by Reason.[3] But the corruption of man-made law by Meed suggests, if it does not symbolize, Meed's corruption of divine law. And in fact the narrative and the

4. I.1–II.50.
5. D. W. Robertson, "The Doctrine of Charity in Medieval Literary Gardens: A Topical Approach through Symbolism and Allegory," *Speculum*, 26 (1951), 24.
6. I.45, 56, 70, 83, 85, 133, 135, 205–6. See the discussion of *temporalia* in Robertson and Huppé, *Scriptural Tradition*, pp. 38–48, for some of the Church's teachings on the subject.
7. I.3; II.7–17. There is an interesting discussion of Lady Meed's clothing in Robertson and Huppé, pp. 50–2.
8. II.32–5.
9. II.58–63, 163–4, etc.
1. III.12–25.
2. IV.47–103, esp. 94–103.
3. IV.113–48.

speeches are constantly reaching out to show the evil influence of Lady
Meed in other aspects of human life. Most striking is the scene where
Meed corrupts the friars and the sacrament of confession.[4] In his
speech rejecting Lady Meed, Conscience attacks her as a universally
destructive force, not as a corrupter of law alone; and he analyzes
meed as the cause of the damnation of human souls and contrasts it
with another kind of meed, salvation. This larger implication of the
Lady Meed episode is evident in what might be called the poet's text
for the vision, the 15th Psalm (14th in the Vulgate):

> Domine quis habitabit in tabernaculo tuo? aut quis requiescet in
> monte sancto tuo? Qui ingreditur sine macula, et operatur iusti-
> tiam: Qui loquitur veritatem in corde suo, qui non egit dolum in
> lingua sua: Nec fecit proximo suo malum, et opprobrium non
> accepit aduersus proximos suos. Ad nihilum deductus est in con-
> spectu eius malignus: timentes autem Dominum glorificat: Qui
> iurat proximo suo, et non decipit, qui pecuniam suam non dedit
> ad vsuram, et munera super innocentem non accepit: Qui facit
> haec, non mouebitur in aeternum.[5]

The issue in the Lady Meed episode, therefore, is more than political
and legal reform. The issue is salvation, and worldly reward is condemned because it leads to damnation. The conclusion of the episode,
in which Wrong is punished and Meed is driven out by Conscience
and Reason,[6] preaches the lesson that mankind can control the desire
for worldly reward and check the drift toward damnation by following
the dictates of conscience and reason. In this way man will keep the
divine law. At the same time he will keep man-made law. (The machinery of law, and the king himself, must be ruled by these faculties
of reason and conscience.) Both Conscience and Reason in their
speeches before the king describe the day when meed no longer rules
as an era of universal peace and love, in which the divine law of love
will be maintained on earth:

> Shal na more Mede · be maistre, as she is nouthe,
> Ac loue and lowenesse · and lewte togederes,
> Thise shul be maistres on molde · treuthe to saue.[7]

The second vision of the *Visio* shows how the field of folk can begin
to follow Truth and move toward salvation. First there must be repentance, the necessary prologue to all right action. Repentance comes

---

4. III.35–63.
5. The edition of the Vulgate used in this essay is *Biblia Sacra Vulgatae Editionis,*
ed. P. Michael Hetzenauer, 2d ed., revised, Ratisbon and Rome, 1922.
6. IV.171–95.
7. III.288–90. For the whole passage see 282–322.

in response to the voice of reason, which exhorts man to mend his ways, perform dutifully the tasks to which God has called him in this world, and follow Truth.[8] Repentance's work is the great confession of the deadly sins, where man's evil ways are spread before him until he weeps for forgiveness, promises to reform, and begs to know the way to Truth.[9]

The confession scene is dramatic rather than doctrinal. Its vivid portraits and realistic sketches of medieval life have made it a grab-bag of quotations for the social historian. The long scene does more than illustrate and entertain, however. Lady Meed's scandalous career was a vision of cupidity; the confession scene is larger in scope than this: its theme is sinfulness. Cupidity may be at the root of all or much of this sinfulness, but the confessions reveal, not cupidity alone, but sin in all its variety. At the same time the scene individualizes sinfulness and roots it in the human heart. Without the confession of the deadly sins, the appeal to individual reform which follows would lack emotional power, and the move from the negative first vision to the positive second, from "do not evil" to "do well," would be anticlimax. It is a vision of evil work to motivate and balance the summons to good work of Piers the Plowman.

The confessions testify to the need for forgiveness and reform. Repentance's prayer at the close of the confessional contains the poet's double hope for mankind: God's mercy and love for man, and man's close kinship with God, the semidivinity of human nature coexistent with its sinfulness.

"Now god," quod he, "that of thi goodnesse · gonne the worlde make,
  And of nauȝte madest auȝte · and man moste liche to thi-selue,

> .   .   .   .   .

And madest thi-self with thi sone · and vs synful yliche,

> .   .   .   .   .

And sith with thi self sone · in owre sute deydest. . . .

> .   .   .   .   .

And al that Marke hath ymade · Mathew, Iohan, and Lucas,
Of thyne douȝtiest dedes · were don in owre armes;
  Verbum caro factum est, et habitauit in nobis.
And bi so moche, me semeth · the sikerere we mowe
Bydde and biseche · if it be thi wille,
That art owre fader and owre brother · be merciable to vs." [1]

8. v.11–60.
9. v.61–519.
1. v.488–9, 494, 495, 507–11.

Thirty lines later Piers the Plowman, the symbol of man's semidivine nature, makes his first appearance in the poem to show mankind God's way. Piers knows the way to Truth: Meekness, obedience to conscience, and good deeds, especially the observance of the ten commandments, lead to Truth's castle; grace enables one to enter; and if grace be lacking, entrance may be secured through the mercy of Christ and Mary.[2] But before man can begin his journey toward Truth he must do his feudal duties in this world [3]—an obligation he is often reluctant to perform.[4] Although hunger drives the lazy and rebellious to labor, it vanishes with the harvest and they return to idleness.[5] To Piers and to all men who do perform their duties, however, Truth grants a pardon:

> Et qui bona egerunt, ibunt in vitam eternam;
> Qui vero mala, in ignem eternum.[6]

Like the first vision with its picture of legal corruption, the second vision presents a problem in the poet's own world and time, the problem of feudal duties and labor. His interest in this problem is real and intense. But like the first vision, the second vision also gives this immediate issue a spiritual significance. The good work of this world is also in some measure the good work of salvation. The poet's method is not symbolic. At most, the scene of the plowing of the half-acre is suggestive of this value. The faithful laborers in the field may suggest —certainly they parallel rather than contradict—the image of the man of good works. But the scene is to be read literally.[7] The poet treats the issues of feudal duty, rebellious laborers, beggars, and famine with the passion of an inspired pamphleteer. The vision as a whole is something more than a political poem, not because it has a second meaning, but because the poet also talks of salvation.

The talk about matters spiritual is not extraneous to his doctrine of work. It grows out of his conviction that there is an intimate and indissoluble alliance between labor and spirituality. This conviction is embodied, as I have said, in the figure of Piers himself. It appears again and again in this vision. Truth is attainable only by the faithful laborer; one must faithfully perform his duties in this world before he can do those spiritual works essential for salvation. Piers, the good plowman,

2. v.570–638.
3. VI.3–113.
4. VI.114–72.
5. VI.173–321.
6. VII.1–111. The Latin is given after VII.111.
7. For an allegorical or symbolical interpretation of the scene in the half-acre see Robertson and Huppé, pp. 83–91. I cannot accept this or their other "allegorical" readings of the poem. See Morton W. Bloomfield's review in *Speculum, 27* (1952), 245–9. Robertson and Huppé do, however, quote an interesting passage from Bede (PL, *91*, col. 995) on the necessity of work for salvation (p. 87).

serves Truth, and only he can show mankind the way to Truth.[8] And
before mankind can perform the spiritual work which Piers has described for them, they must join him in work on the half-acre.[9] Truth
grants His pardon only to Piers and those who help him:

> And alle that halpe hym to erie · to sette or to sowe,
> Or any other myster · that myȝte Pieres auaille,
> Pardoun with Pieres plowman · treuthe hath ygraunted.[1]

Was not mankind commanded to labor by God?

The doctrine of the pardon, do well, i.e. do good works and be saved,
is a logical culmination of the doctrine of labor in the vision. It sums
up at the same time a line of thought running through the entire *Visio*.
At the very beginning Holy Church advised man to lead a good life,
in words which are almost a translation of the Latin pardon:

> And alle that worche with wronge · wenden hij shulle
> After her deth day · and dwelle with that shrewe [Lucifer].
> Ac tho that worche wel · as holiwritt telleth,
> And enden as I ere seide · in treuthe, that is the best,
> Mowe be siker that her soule · shal wende to heuene,
> Ther treuthe is in Trinitee · and troneth hem alle.[2]

She further advised kings, knights, rich men, and clergy to conduct
themselves properly if they would follow Truth.[3] Reason gave similar
advice to priests, religious, kings, popes, and lawyers, and less directly
to the common folk.[4] Do well, too, is the lesson of the confession scene.

The meaning of the pardon and the pardon scene, however, has been
a matter of debate and dissension among the critics, largely because of
Piers' quarrel with the priest. The priest tells Piers his pardon is no
pardon at all; and Piers, in anger ("pure tene"), tears up the document.
He quotes from the Psalter and says he will not work so hard to feed
his belly anymore, but make prayers and penance his plow, as the
Psalter and Evangels advise. The priest sneers at his learning, they
quarrel, and the noise awakens the Dreamer, who concludes, after re-
flecting on the scene, that pardons from popes may be of some help,
but Dowel is a more certain way to salvation.[5]

The scene does have its confusing aspects, particularly the priest's
statement that the pardon is no pardon, Piers' action in tearing the
pardon, and his description of the change he proposes to make in his

---

8. v.544–62.
9. Passus VI.
1. VII.6–8.
2. I.126–31 (cf. A.I.117–22 and C.II.130–4).
3. I.94–101 ; 173–201.
4. V.42–60, 24–41.
5. VII.112–200.

mode of life. There have been a variety of interpretations for these difficulties, but there is considerable agreement on two main points: the pardon is not a valid pardon, and Piers' words to the priest contain a rejection of the Active Life for the Contemplative Life. Both points, I believe, are mistaken and misleading.[6] The pardon is valid, and Piers affirms, not the superiority of the Contemplative Life over the Active Life, but, within the Active Life, the doctrine of what I shall call *ne solliciti sitis*.

Those who are skeptical about the pardon say either that it has no real validity or that it is valid only for Piers, not for the rest of mankind.[7] Since the poet's theme was the salvation of mankind, this makes the pardon of only limited value. But there is evidence in the text, apart from Piers' puzzling words and actions, which proves the poet intended his audience to accept the pardon as valid for all men. And Piers' words and actions can be interpreted to confirm, not contradict, this view of the pardon.

I have already pointed out that the message of the pardon, do well, is a logical culmination of the doctrine of labor and good works preached throughout the *Visio*. If the pardon is no pardon, if do well is not the way to salvation, the reader has been led down the garden path by a most irresponsible poet. The objection of some critics that the *Visio*, although it may teach that doing good merits salvation, also shows mankind incapable of good works, simply will not hold. They have been blinded by the moralist's inevitable practice of preaching more about men's sins than about their virtues. There are good men in the field of folk and in the scene of the plowing of the half-acre; and the long account of the kinds of men to whom the pardon applies is pointless if the poet believes mankind incapable of goodness. Piers Plowman himself is a symbol of man's capacity for good. Finally, the text leaves no doubt that the Dreamer himself accepts the pardon. If the poet had wanted to strip the pardon of its value, he would hardly have

6. I have reviewed at greater length the various views concerning the Pardon Scene in "The Pardon Scene in *Piers Plowman*," *Speculum, 26* (1951), 317–31.

7. Skepticism about the value of the pardon is expressed in one form or another by the following critics: Wells, "Construction," 124–5, 131. Chambers, *Mind,* pp. 119, 121. Coghill, *MedAev, 2,* 117–18, and *The Pardon,* pp. 17–19. George Winchester Stone, "An Interpretation of the A-Text of *Piers Plowman*," *PMLA, 53* (1938), 666. Francis A. R. Carnegy, *The Relations between the Social and Divine Order in William Langland's "Vision of William Concerning Piers the Plowman"* (Breslau, 1934), pp. 17–18, 44. John Lawlor, "'Piers Plowman': The Pardon Reconsidered," *MLR, 45* (1950), 449–58: Lawlor argues that the *Visio* shows, first, that society can produce only one good man, Piers, and second, it shows through the pardon how far that good man falls short of the standard enjoined upon all men, "Be ye perfect." The tearing of the pardon is an act of acceptance; it shows Piers aware of his imperfection and resolved to pursue a better life, the Contemplative. Robertson and Huppé, pp. 92–4, find the pardon valid; they interpret it as the grace of the Redemption. They go so far beyond the text, however, that I cannot follow them.

ended the *Visio* with the Dreamer's words of acceptance. It is, he says,
a pardon "alle the peple to conforte." [8] Although he expresses the conventional doubts about the trustworthiness of dreams, and worries over
the relative value of papal indulgences and good works, he concludes
that dreams can reveal the truth and that doing well is superior to indulgences. With a bow to orthodoxy he concedes some value to pardons
from Rome, but concludes,

> Ac to trust to thise triennales · trewly me thinketh,
> Is nouȝt so syker for the soule · certis, as is Dowel.
>
> .   .   .   .   .
>
> For-thi I conseille alle Cristene · to crye god mercy,
> And Marie his moder · be owre mene bitwene,
> That god gyue vs grace here · ar we gone hennes,
> Suche werkes to werche · while we ben here,
> That after owre deth-day · Dowel reherce,
> At the day of dome · we dede as he hiȝte.[9]

This is the way the *Visio* ends, with a bang, not with a whimper. There
are no doubts here. The pardon is valid : all men should heed it.

This evidence of the text is supported by the authority which the
pardon possessed. It is not only that the pardon was given by Truth
(and by Truth, as the poem makes clear, is meant God). The lines of
the pardon come from the well-known Athanasian Creed.[1] Popular because of the succinctness with which it stated the essential beliefs of the
Church,[2] the Creed answers in forthright fashion the question which
the poem itself seeks to answer : What shall a man do to be saved :
"Quicumque vult salvus esse" are the words which open the Creed ;
and immediately after the article which is quoted as Piers' pardon in
the poem, the thirty-ninth, the Creed closes with a blunt assertion of
its authority : "Haec est fides catholica : quam nisi quisque fideliter
firmiterque crediderit : salvus esse non poterit." [3]

Although the poet did not say the pardon came from the Athanasian
Creed, the Creed was so well-known there can be little doubt that both
he and his audience knew the source. The Creed was not only a creed
but also a part of the liturgy and was actually considered a psalm,
known familiarly as the "Quicumque vult." It was recited as part of
the service at Prime, and was as familiar as the Psalms to the poet

---

8. VII.146. Not in A. In C.x.300 it is "the puple to gladen."
9. VII.179–80, 195–200.
1. First noted by Burdach, *Ackermann*, p. 267, n. 1.
2. Cf. J. Tixeront, "Athanase (Symbole de Saint)," *DTC*, I, Pt. II, 2186–7.
3. For the Latin text of the Creed see Philip Schaff, *Creeds of Christendom* (New
York, 1877), *2*, 66–70.

and his contemporaries.[4] There was also a Middle English translation of the Creed.[5] Finally, there is some evidence that the particular lines of the Creed quoted as Piers' pardon may have had, as Nevill Coghill suggests, "some vogue as a catch-phrase about salvation towards the end of the fourteenth century and a little later." [6] They were used, he points out, at the climax of the last scene of the *Castle of Perseverance*.[7]

This evidence both within and outside of the text is not canceled out by Piers' reactions in the Pardon Scene. To argue that it is would ascribe to these reactions more importance than they deserve. The fact that they are dropped completely in the C-text [8] suggests that the essential meaning of the scene is communicated without them. An unquestionably dramatic passage was removed because it was confusing. To the Dreamer, even in B, Piers' reactions do not bear the message of the scene. He comments on them not at all, only on the pardon and the priest's impugning of it. The only issue for the Dreamer is the one raised by the priest's rejection of the pardon: which gives greater promise of salvation, the good life or papal indulgences.

But, although one may deny that Piers' reactions carry the principal message of the scene, there is no denying their presence in A and B. What, therefore, do these reactions mean? If Piers is rejecting the pardon, the rejection can only be the poet's way of showing how the Church's practice of selling indulgences leads men astray, a point he wants to make.[9] The view that Piers rejects the pardon has, however, this great difficulty: it contradicts the main purpose of the scene and the symbolic value already given Piers. As the Dreamer's comments reveal, the purpose of the scene is to advocate doing well and to

---

4. The frequency with which it was recited at Prime varied according to custom. The Symbolum Athanasium is used at Prime on Sundays in the Roman Rite, daily at Prime in many Roman derivatives (e.g. the Sarum) and in the Ambrosian Rite: Henry Jenner, "Creed, Liturgical Use of," in *The Catholic Encyclopedia* (New York, 1913), 4, 479. According to the Sarum Breviary it was recited daily except from Maundy Thursday to the end of Easter Week: William Chatterley Bishop, "A Plain Introduction to the Structure and Arrangement of the Salisbury Breviary," *Breviarium ad Usum Insignis Ecclesiae Sarum* (Cambridge, England, 1882–86), *3*, xxxi. In the Psalterium of the York Breviary the Creed is prefaced with these instructions: "dicitur de feria: vel ferialiter de dominica." *Breviarium ad Usum Insignis Ecclesie Eboracensis*, Publications of the Surtees Society, *71* (Durham, 1880), 1, 882.

5. See George Hickes, *Linguarum Vett. Septentrionalium Thesaurus* . . . (Oxford, 1703–05), 1, 233–5; and W. Heuser, "Eine Vergessene Handschrift des Surteespsalters und die dort eingeschalteten Mittelenglischen Gedichte," *Anglia, 29* (1906), 405–8.

6. *The Pardon,* p. 19, n. 2.

7. *The Macro Plays,* ed. F. J. Furnivall and A. W. Pollard, EETS, e.s. *91* (London, 1904), 186. Cf. also the use of the lines in a fourteenth-century sermon: *Sermons,* p. 29.

8. Cf. C.x.284–94.

9. Cf. R. W. Chambers, "Long Will, Dante, and the Righteous Heathen," *Essays and Studies by Members of the English Association, 9* (Oxford, 1924), 53: "When the priest, representing current ideas, refuses to accept it [the pardon], the poet is brought up against the contrast which he feels so bitterly, between his own sense of justice, and that which seems to him to prevail in the current practice of the Church."

attack papal indulgences. The priest supports indulgences. To give the priest a convert weakens the poet's attack. And to make the convert Piers, the symbol of right conduct, the follower of Truth, confuses the message and destroys the value of Piers as a symbol. Also, this would put Piers on the priest's side at one moment, but at loggerheads with him a moment later. And in C Piers opposes the priest and so supports the pardon. The view that Piers accepts the pardon creates too many difficulties to be tenable.

Piers' reactions, as a matter of fact, can be interpreted to signify his acceptance of the pardon. The act of tearing the pardon, so often understood as an act of rejection, implies this only so long as one disregards the special nature of his pardon. When Coghill and Chambers say that Piers decides not to put his trust in a piece of parchment, to bulls with seals,[1] they overlook something. Just as Piers' Testament is not really a will but a device for communicating an ethical message dramatically by means of the contrast between the conventional form and its novel content, so too the pardon is not really an orthodox pardon but a device for stating an ethical principle dramatically. The clash between form and content is even sharper here, for this pardon contains a message which is by implication an attack on pardons and which does in fact lead to such an attack by the Dreamer. How, then, can we speak of it as we would of a conventional pardon, as a piece of parchment, a bull with seals. That is precisely what it is not. In accepting its message, Piers is rejecting bulls with seals. In tearing the parchment, Piers is symbolically tearing paper pardons from Rome. One had to possess such pardons to receive their supposed benefits. But this pardon, once its message has been read and taken to heart, has served its purpose and is only a worthless piece of paper. (And so, the implication may be, are all pardons. The poet could not afford to condemn pardons too overtly.) Piers has lost nothing by tearing it. The act, then, because of the special character of the pardon, was intended as a sign that Piers had rejected indulgences and accepted the command to do well. Unfortunately, it was a very confusing sign.[2]

1. *Mind*, p. 119; *The Pardon*, pp. 17–20.
2. Glunz, *Literarästhetik*, p. 529, says the pardon serves a double function in the poem. It indicates to the various classes in the ploughing scene that they are on the right road, in which each serves the community. Piers symbolizes the perfect man, who satisfies the common weal as well as the individual good. But Piers tears the pardon at the moment when this first goal is reached. He has fulfilled one command to do good, to do good for the community. Now he hears another command to do good: to prove his worth as an individual in personal righteousness. The tearing of the pardon signifies the end of one condition and the beginning of another for Piers. Glunz' reading seems an accurate description of the direction in which the poem is moving at this point. I would object only to his confining the issue in the second vision to the economic good of the community—the salvation of mankind is the implicit issue of the second vision. And I would object to his reading so much into the simple act of tearing the pardon, especially when the action is omitted in C. The action, it seems to me, must be related to the issue of the relative value of pardons and good works.

Once the act of tearing the pardon is seen as no act of rejection, Piers' other reactions can easily be explained to imply acceptance of the pardon. Piers' "tene" may be directed against himself, as Chambers suggests: he may be vexed to discover that he has wasted precious time being busy about his belly-joy.[3] But it is more reasonable to assume that it is directed against the priest. He is angry with him a few lines later. And the poet is angry with him, the supporter of papal indulgences, the misleader of souls. The priest is the one logical object in the scene for Piers' anger.

Piers' words also support the pardon. His quotation from the Psalter, " 'si ambulauero in medio vmbre mortis, non timebo mala; quoniam tu mecum es' " (Psalm XXII in the Vulgate), was interpreted by several medieval glosses as an affirmation of faith, and it is certain the poet knew a gloss on the line.[4] Although there are several glosses on the verse, the one he most probably knew was that which appears in both the *Glossa Ordinaria* and in Peter Lombard's *Commentarius in Psalmos Davidos.*[5] It interprets "mecum es" as meaning (following Augustine), "In corde per fidem, ut post umbram mortis ego tecum sim." The poet clearly associates the verse with the idea of reward to the faithful man, for when he quotes it again at B.XII.289, it comes after a discussion of men of steadfast belief; and immediately preceding the verse is another Latin line: "Deus dicitur quasi dans vitam eternam suis, hoc est, fidelibus." If the line is an expression of Piers' firm faith, what is Piers resolved to have faith in? If the line has any relevance to the dramatic situation in which it occurs, it must mean either that Piers will have faith in the priest or that he will have faith in the pardon. The poet would hardly have Piers quote the Psalter to support papal indulgences. There is no difficulty if he quotes it in support of the Athanasian Creed. He is resolved to have faith in the pardon, in spite of the priest's objections. Faith, for the poet, always meant what the pardon preached: moral action, doing well. So he has Piers announce at once that he will do prayers and penance, which would be considered good works,[6] and which imply a rejection of papal indulgences.

If the pardon is valid and Piers accepts it, then the way of life he proceeds to describe and which he determines to follow is the "do well" enjoined by the pardon:

"I shal cessen of my sowyng," quod Pieres · "and swynk nouʒt so harde,
Ne about my bely-ioye · so bisi be namore!

---

3. *Mind*, p. 121.
4. R. W. Chambers pointed out that the poet quotes the same verse at B.XII.289, and adds, " 'The glose graunteth vpon that vers a gret mede to treuthe. . . .' ": "Incoherencies in the A- and B-texts of 'Piers Plowman' and Their Bearing on the Authorship," *London Mediaeval Studies*, I (1937), 34.
5. PL, *113*, col. 876; PL, *191*, col. 243.
6. Cf. Dunning, p. 147.

Of preyers and of penaunce · my plow shal ben herafter,
And wepen whan I shulde slepe · though whete-bred me faille.
The prophete his payn ete · in penaunce and in sorwe,
By that the sauter seith · so dede other manye;
That loueth god lelly · his lyflode is ful esy:
    Fuerunt michi lacrime mee panes die ac nocte.
And, but if Luke lye · he lereth vs bi foules,
We shulde nouȝt be to bisy · aboute the worldes blisse;
Ne solliciti sitis · he seyth in the gospel,
And sheweth vs bi ensamples · vs selue to wisse.
The foules on the felde · who fynt hem mete at wynter?
Haue thei no gernere to go to · but god fynt hem alle." [7]

Just what kind of life is described here? A good many critics, as I have
mentioned, say this is the Contemplative Life, to which Piers is turning
from the Active Life. The view depends in part on the assumption that
the pardon is rejected. It rests also on several other assumptions, all of
them mistaken.

First, there is the assumption that Dowel is the kind of bodily labor
seen in the plowing scene. Since Piers says that hereafter he will not
do so much bodily work, he must be rejecting Dowel and moving on
to Dobet (and it is assumed that Dobet is the life of contemplation).
But the poet never calls bodily labor "Dowel." He uses the phrase for
the first time when the priest translates the pardon and when the
Dreamer comments on its message. So Dowel must be something more
than bodily labor. (Also, it is unreasonable to assume the poet has Piers
move on to something better than Dowel at the very moment when the
reader first hears about Dowel.)

There is also the assumption that Piers is abandoning bodily labor
completely. As Father Dunning observed, Piers "does not say that he
will work no more: he merely says he will not work *so hard,* nor be
so busy about providing himself with means of sustenance. . . . Piers
merely declares that he will give the interests of his soul a decided
preference over the interests of the body." [8]

There has been, as I have already observed, some misunderstanding
of the nature of the Active and the Contemplative Life among the
students who have seen these lives as major patterns in the poem.
The misunderstanding appears in their interpretation of this speech.
The prayers and penance which Piers says he will perform do not prove
that he is taking up the Contemplative Life. Prayers and penance are
not confined to contemplatives, nor do they distinguish the Contempla-

7. VII.117–29.
8. *Piers Plowman*, p. 149. Father Dunning has a sound analysis of the Pardon Scene
(pp. 145–52), except that he tries to establish that the priest accepts the pardon.

tive Life from the Active. In Walter Hilton's *Epistle on Mixed Life,* "bodely werkes," the appropriate religious activities of those leading the Active Life ("worldly men & wymen the whiche lefully vsen worldly goodes, & wylfully vsen worldly besynes"), are contrasted with the activities of contemplatives. These "bodely werkes" include "al maner of god werkis þat thy soule doth by þe wyttes & þe membris of thy body," such as fasting, waking, restraining of fleshly lusts by doing penance, doing deeds of bodily or spiritual mercy to one's fellow Christians, and suffering bodily harm for the love of righteousness.[9] The program for those in the Active Life recommended in Hilton's piece *On Daily Work* is even more rigorous.[1] The Active Life, then, is not physical labor, but just the kind of activity that Piers pledges himself to: prayers and care for his spiritual profit. Of the contemplative's withdrawal from the world, being quiet from outward action, and hope to see the face of God there is no hint in Piers' speech.

Perhaps it is not quite accurate to say that the Active Life is "just the kind of activity that Piers pledges himself to." It is, however, a way of life that can be realized within the Active Life. I cannot agree with Chambers when he says Piers' determination not to worry about food any longer is "the Contemplative Life as Walter Hilton defines it: when men forsake 'all business, charges, and government of worldly goods, and make themselves poor and naked to the bare need of the bodily kind. . . .' "[2] The doctrine which Piers states is the doctrine of *ne solliciti sitis,* not of the Contemplative Life. The Gospel passages Piers quotes were not interpreted as a summons to the Contemplative Life. According to the *Glossa Ordinaria,* the verses say, not that man shall not labor, but that he shall not be *too solicitous* about his food: "non prohibet providentiam, per quam in sudore vultus panis praeparatur, sed vetat sollicitudinem quae mentem perturbat et ab aeternis revocat."[3] God will provide for the righteous man, even as he has provided for the fowls of the air: "Qui dedit majora, id est vitam et corpus, dabit et minora, id est victum et vestes. In his promissis veritatis nemo dubitet: Sit homo quod esse debet, mox adduntur ei omnia propter quem sunt facta."[4] The *Catena Aurea* expresses precisely the meaning of the lines: "Be not withdrawn by temporal cares from things eternal."[5]

The line comes from the Sermon on the Mount, which is, if not the

9. *Yorkshire Writers, I,* 264–6. Father Dunning has material showing that the command to do good refers to "the good works of a virtuous life." *Piers Plowman,* pp. 146–7.
1. *Yorkshire Writers, I,* 137–56.
2. *Mind,* p. 124.
3. On Luke xii: 22: PL, *114,* col. 296.
4. On Matthew vi: 25: PL, *114,* cols. 105–6.
5. I, 251. See also Dunning, *Piers Plowman,* pp. 148–51.

source of several of the leading ideas in the poem, at least the authority the poet appealed to in support of them—the *Beati pauperes* of the *Beatitudes* for the doctrine of poverty, *fiat voluntas tua* from the Pater noster for the same doctrine and for *ne solliciti sitis, dimitte nobis debita nostra* from the Pater noster for the doctrine of *redde quod debes*.[6] The passage in the Sermon where *ne solliciti sitis* appears states the injunction at great length and with considerable power:

> Ideo dico vobis, ne soliciti sitis animae vestrae quid manducetis, neque corpori vestro quid induamini. Nonne anima plus est quam esca: et corpus plus quam vestimentum? Respicite volatilia caeli, quoniam non serunt, neque metunt, neque congregant in horrea: et pater vester caelestis pascit illa. Nonne vos magis pluris estis illis? Quis autem vestrum cogitans potest adiicere ad staturam suam cubitum unum? Et de vestimento quid soliciti estis? Considerate lilia agri quomodo crescunt: non laborant, neque nent. Dico autem vobis, quoniam nec Salomon in omni gloria sua coopertus est sicut unum ex istis. Si autem foenum agri, quod hodie est, et cras in clibanum mittitur, Deus sic vestit: quanto magis vos modicae fidei? Nolite ergo soliciti esse, dicentes: Quid manducabimus, aut quid bibemus, aut quo operiemur? haec enim omnia gentes inquirunt. Scit enim pater vester, quia his omnibus indigetis. Quaerite ergo primum regnum Dei, et iustitiam eius: et haec omnia adiicientur vobis. Nolite ergo soliciti esse in crastinum. Crastinus enim dies solicitus erit sibiipsi. sufficit diei malitia sua.[7]

Sollicitudo, as Konrad Burdach has pointed out, was a catchword of Christian ethics. It is the continual concern for worldly goods, greediness for gain, avarice.[8] Burdach's investigation of the doctrine of *ne solliciti sitis* in the Old and New Testament and in Augustine and later medieval religious thinkers proves the doctrine was not peculiar to the *Piers Plowman* poet.[9] He further shows that the doctrine, together with the doctrine of poverty preached more explicitly in *Dowel,* was associated with the idealization of labor, not with the Contemplative Life.[1] *Ne solliciti sitis* was for the poet the solution to a fundamental question: how to provide for the body without destroying the soul.

6. For *Beati pauperes* cf. xiv.214; for *fiat voluntas tua* cf. xiv.48 and xv.174; for *ne solliciti sitis* cf. xiv.33; for *dimitte nobis debita nostra* cf. xix.384–92.

7. Matthew vi.

8. *Ackermann*, p. 270.

9. Ibid., pp. 268, 269–83, 308–10, 310 n. 2, 351–8. See also the quotation from Wyclif, p. 306, n. 1.

1. Ibid., pp. 294 (point three, on the cult of poverty and Wyclif's poor priests), 294–6 (point six, on the moral duty of active work), 295–6, n. 1 (the quotation from Wyclif), 351–4. The doctrine of the importance of work appears in the arguments against the begging friars. Cf. Richard Fitzralph's *Defensio,* pp. 86–7, 88–9, 89–90.

The answer is: Care for the soul, and God will provide if necessary for the body. The essence of the doctrine, Burdach says, is that a faithful devotion to God, an inner freedom from care about gain, and an easy mind which calculates nothing must be the basis of all work and all activity which merits God's grace. It alone gives the soul the serenity and the power to love which is due man as God's image, and which leads him to God.[2]

This doctrine will appear at greater length in the visions which follow. What Piers says here is the merest hint, a preparation for the fuller development to come in *Dowel,* especially at its climax, the scene with Haukyn. That is why the Dreamer does not mention it after the vision ends, and why it could be dropped in C. It is the first glimpse of Dowel, the first suggestion of what Piers' pardon means. The poet quite properly concentrates, as the *Visio* ends, not on this foreshadowing, but on the merit of the pardon, Dowel's superiority over indulgences. As we have seen, there is no denial of the pardon. It is valid for mankind, and Piers accepts its message. It states the basic rule that man must follow if he would be saved. This rule is that he must do well. The rule is stated in a form (the unorthodox pardon) designed to show the falseness of the contrary view, that man can purchase salvation. The attack in the Pardon Scene on the philosophy of money applied to the scheme of salvation is paralleled and to some extent prepared for by the attack on the philosophy of money applied to the social order in the Lady Mede episode. Similarly, the support in the plowing scene of the philosophy of work applied to the social order parallels and prepares for the support of the philosophy of work applied here to the scheme of salvation. For the pardon says man must "work" (do well) to be saved, and it is offered to, and accepted by, the personification of the good workman, Piers Plowman. The doctrine of the spiritual value of physical labor blurs the line between "work" and "good work" and makes them a unity. The way to Truth, which Piers described for the pilgrims, involved activities ethical and religious in nature; but first the half-acre must be plowed. This prerequisite of "work" having been described, the poem proceeds in *Dowel, Dobet, and Dobest* to an examination of the *good* work, which, together with work, leads to salvation. The *Visio* has dramatized the principles of good and evil and shown a sick society which needs to be purged and reformed. The remainder of the poem will show what man must do in order to do good, and how he is able to do it—that is to say, it will convey the poet's view of the scheme of salvation.

2. *Ackermann,* pp. 351–2.

4

"Dowel, Dobet, and Dobest the Third"

TO ALL of the poem after the *Visio* the poet gave the title
Dowel, Dobet, and Dobest. In the A-text it was called the *Vita
de Dowel, Dobet, and Dobest.*[1] This was the section he subsequently expanded until he had almost tripled the length of his poem;
and in the B-text and C-text he divided this section into three parts and
called the first part *Dowel,*[2] the second part *Dobet,*[3] and the third part
Dobest.[4] Exactly what he meant by these titles is one of the questions
that should be answered in an explanation of the poem. The question
would be difficult enough to answer in itself, but the poet introduced a
further complication. Throughout the *Vita* in A and throughout *Dowel*
in B and C the poet also employed the terms "Dowel," "Dobet," and
"Dobest" in his text. "Employed" is a mild word. They are a kind of
maddening refrain. The Dreamer, who has learned in the Pardon Scene
that doing well is essential for salvation, asks a variety of personifications where or what are Dowel, Dobet, and Dobest. The repetition of
the terms is not all that is maddening. The answer to the Dreamer's
question would seem to be a matter of considerable importance, for the
answer will apparently reveal what man must do to be saved. But no
satisfactory answer seems ever to emerge. No two characters agree in
their explanation. Dowel is variously defined as truly wedded folk,
to believe in the articles of the faith, contrition of heart, etc. The definitions of Dobet and Dobest are equally varied. The poet gives no final
summary of the definitions, nor does he indicate which explanation is
correct. He seems completely unaware that anything of the sort would
be expected of him.

What is the significance of this multiplicity of definitions, and what
are the meanings of the terms Dowel, Dobet, and Dobest? Do the defini-

---

1. Cf. the colophon at the end of A.VIII. The *Vita* title is often carelessly applied
to *Dowel, Dobet, and Dobest* in B and C, and may influence scholars to search for
"lives" or "ways of life." But the *Vita* title, however convenient as a title for this
part of the poem, was dropped by the poet from B and C. Where it is found in B or
C MSS, Chambers established, it is clearly the work of scribes copying it into the
B or C text from their knowledge of an A MS: "The Original Form of the A-Text,"
MLR, 6 (1911), 313.
2. B.VIII–XIV; C.XI–XVII.
3. B.XV–XVIII; C.XVIII–XXI.
4. B.XIX–XX; C.XXII–XXIII.

34

tions contradict one another? Does each definition move a step forward toward a final, correct explanation? Can the explanations for each term be reduced to a general definition which will harmonize all the explanations? And what is the relation between the explanations for the terms and the section titles? Must the explanations of Dowel harmonize with the theme of *Dowel,* those for Dobet with the theme of *Dobet,* those for Dobest with the theme of *Dobest?* "If any wight would tell me what Dowel, Dobet, and Dobest were," the Dreamer says to Imaginatif, "I would never work again, but wend to holy church and there bid my beads, except to eat or sleep." Amen, says the baffled reader.

Earlier criticism paid little attention to this problem. Skeat did not mention it. Jusserand did it less than justice by remarking that "Dowel, Dobet and Dobest have two or three different meanings." He solved the difficulty by arbitrarily choosing one set of definitions as correct: *Disce, Doce, Dilige.*[5] This summary solution has been repeated by G. G. Coulton [6] and John Matthews Manly.[7]

The German scholar Otto Mensendieck faced the problems of the terms directly. He was convinced the poet intended to explain them, though he confessed the answers were curiously varied. The difficulties, he believed, disappeared if one understood that *Dowel* presented the poet's ethical and religious development.[8] The varied explanations reflect his changing attitudes as he matured.[9] Mensendieck suggested that originally the poet believed in the conventional medieval doctrine of three moral states, Active, Contemplative, and Episcopal, but that ultimately he discarded this view and at the end of *Dowel* gave only one way of life for all men: be followers of Christ in poverty and love.[1] Mensendieck believed, therefore, that there was no connection between the definitions of Dobet and Dobest and the *Dobet* and *Dobest* sections. *Dobet* and *Dobest* are elaborations on the single, ultimate principle of moral action provided at the conclusion of *Dowel.* This explanation (which need not depend on Mensendieck's autobiographical thesis) resolves a number of puzzling features in the text, but it has been generally ignored.

Henry W. Wells some years later attacked this problem of the terms. He found over-all meanings for Dowel, Dobet, and Dobest and related their meanings to the *Dowel, Dobet,* and *Dobest* sections. The explana-

5. J. J. Jusserand, *Piers Plowman: A Contribution to the History of English Mysticism,* trans. M. E. R., revised and enlarged by the author (London, T. Fisher Unwin, 1894), pp. 155, 185.

6. *Medieval Panorama: The English Scene from Conquest to Reformation* (Cambridge, England, 1938), p. 538.

7. "'Piers the Plowman' and Its Sequence," in *The Cambridge History of English Literature* (New York and Cambridge, England, 1908), 2, 32.

8. *Charakterentwickelung,* pp. 8–9.

9. Ibid., p. 15.

1. Ibid., pp. 53–6, 57 f.

tions of Dowel define the Active Life, pictured in *Dowel;* those for
Dobet define the Contemplative Life, pictured in *Dobet;* those for
Dobest define the Mixed or Episcopal Life, pictured in *Dobest.*[2] Coghill
and Chambers accepted, with modifications, Wells' explanation of the
terms and titles. Coghill has written, "Langland's definitions . . . are
cumulative [his italics]. . . . Each restatement may be taken as a new
slant of thought upon the same idea, a succession of facets cut upon
the same stone." [3] All the definitions of one term, according to this view,
add up to a description of a single way of life, and the general definition of each term is related to that section of the poem for which the
term is used as a title.

I believe, however, that these assumptions are not supported by the
text, that the definitions are not "cumulative," and that the statements
about any one term do not add up to a way of life. Dowel, Dobet, and
Dobest are not "terms," each with a fixed meaning, but are rather
divisions of the generic term "Dowel." It follows that there is no relation between the explanations of Dobet and the *Dobet* section or between those for Dobest and the *Dobest* section, because the terms Dobet
and Dobest have no one meaning which those sections can dramatize.
This conclusion is similar to Mensendieck's, though it is not based on
all his premises.

There are two particular difficulties in Wells' theory. First, the poet
never gives any final statement about Dobet and Dobest. Yet the many
explanations of the words make such a summing up an absolute necessity if they possessed an over-all meaning he wished his readers to
understand. His failure to provide this summing up suggests he had no
over-all meaning in mind. (For Dowel there is a kind of final definition. In the scene in the real world which begins *Dowel,* before the com-
plicating terms Dobet and Dobest have been introduced, the friars tell
the Dreamer that Dowel is charity.[4] And throughout *Dowel,* as elsewhere in the poem, charity, the law of love, is preached. When *Dowel*
has come to a close, the Dreamer still desires a "kynde knowyng" of
Dowel. In the opening of the first vision of *Dobet,* Soul appears and
teaches the Dreamer about charity.[5] This may not be a completely satisfactory handling of Dowel, but nothing comparable exists for Dobet
and Dobest.)

A second difficulty is that some of the explanations cannot be related
to "a way of life." For example, Conscience says that Dowel, Dobet,
and Dobest are contrition, confession, and satisfaction, respectively.[6]

2. "Construction," 123–40.
3. *MedAev, 2,* 128.
4. VIII.45–6.
5. XV.1–2, 145 ff.
6. XIV.18–23.

But how is "satisfaction" particularly related to the authoritative life (the over-all meaning of Dobest according to Wells and Coghill) or any way of life? It is simply the third and completing part of the process of penance. Nor can Conscience's definitions of Dowel and Dobet be related to "ways of life." Coghill says these particular definitions are "not so much a doctrine as an analogy." [7] But what is the analogy? Other definitions also cannot be very convincingly ascribed to a way of life. [8]

The poet, I believe, used the triad Dowel, Dobet, and Dobest, not as a set of terms, but as a literary device to elaborate his meaning. He used the triad to express the divisions of the idea contained in the generic term Dowel as he first used it in the poem: Dowel is the good life that leads to salvation. Because the personifications vary in their capacity to inform the Dreamer, and because various activities considered good fall into two or three parts, statements about Dowel are sometimes broken into two parts (Dowel and Dobet) or into three (Dowel, Dobet, and Dobest). If Conscience tells the Dreamer about penance as a necessary part of the good life, he must observe the three-fold division of penance and tell him about contrition, confession, and satisfaction. The threefold division of ideas in medieval thought is, of course, a commonplace. Moreover, there are degrees of effort in the struggle to lead the good life. And the triad Dowel, Dobet, and Dobest is, after all, a comparison of the adverb "wel" and therefore represents degrees of effectiveness in the effort to "do well."

As evidence that the triad is an elaboration of what is contained in the generic term Dowel, consider first the contrast between the first mention of Dowel and the first mention of the triad. Dowel's introduction is dramatic. It comes in the Pardon Scene after considerable suspense has been created about the pardon; the term carries the important message that good deeds rather than indulgences will lead to salvation; and it leads to an explosive argument between Piers and the priest. The triad, on the contrary, is introduced quite casually. The character Thought, asked about Dowel, replies that Dowel, Dobet, and Dobest the third are three fair virtues and not far to find. [9] The triad is mentioned without any preparation and is pointed up by no comment from the Dreamer. The manner of introduction suggests that Dobet and Dobest have no meaning apart from the meaning of the generic term Dowel.

There is the same contrast between Dowel alone and the triad in their final appearances. Except for an isolated passage where it is applied to Christ's life, the triad is last used when Conscience tells Haukyn

7. *MedAev*, 2, 127.
8. E.g., IX.92–7; 199–206.
9. VIII. 78 ff.

that Dowel is contrition, Dobet is confession, and Dobest is satisfaction.[1] There is a reference to Dowel a few lines later, and perhaps an implied reference to the other terms, though they are not used.[2] And in this casual fashion the triad disappears from the poem. There are, however, two more references to Dowel, and both reveal its importance. The first occurs at the conclusion of *Dowel*. Haukyn, moved by Patience's speech on poverty, bewails the fact that after his christening he had not died and been buried "for doweles sake."[3] A few lines later the Dreamer, awakening, says it was a wondrous long time before he could "kyndely knowe what was Dowel."[4] At length, Soul gives him his answer.[5] Significantly, it is of Dowel alone that we hear at the last, not the triad. The triad is abandoned casually, and the poem discusses what it has been discussing all along, Dowel, the good life. Dowel, it should be noticed, begins and ends the inquiry. The triad appears in the midst of the discussion of Dowel and is dropped shortly before it ends. This is difficult to explain if Dobet and Dobest have some significance apart from Dowel.[6]

A study of the manner in which the poet uses the triad also suggests that it is a device for elaborating on the meaning of Dowel. There are several peculiarities to be observed. First, the relationship between the terms and their specifically assigned meanings is very unstable. Second, Dobet or Dobest is sometimes omitted from the triad without any apparent significance attaching to the omission. Third, Dowel is frequently used as a synonym for all three terms.

If the poet had in mind some concept, such as the Active Life, for which Dowel was his term, another concept for Dobet, and another for Dobest, he would be using the terms with the general meaning of each already clearly established. But the relationship between the terms and their meanings is very unstable. The poet has difficulty in assigning meanings to a term in specific situations. Again, he feels free to use the terms at times without any intention to communicate meaning (except their literal meaning). And he will give a meaning to one term and then later assign it to another. Yet if he has in mind a specific,

1. xiv.18–23.
2. xiv.87, 89–94.
3. xiv.320–1.
4. xv.1–2.
5. xv.23 ff., esp. 145 ff., the passage on charity.
6. Both B.xiv.320–1 and B.x̌v.1–2 are omitted in C. But in C, as in B, Dowel takes his final bow alone. The last reference to the triad is at C.xvii.25–36. But at C.xvii.177 the phrase "do wel" is used. Likewise, when the A-text is brought to what is apparently a premature conclusion, Dowel alone is referred to: A.xii.2, 32, 36–7, 54. And cf. the final reference, A.xii.94–5: "'And ther-fore do after Do-wel . whil thi dayes duren, That thi play be plentevous . in paradys with aungelys!'" Part of A.xii is the work of one John But (cf. A.xii.106); how much, is a matter of wide disagreement. See the note on A.xii.117 in *Piers the Plowman: A Critical Edition of the A-Version*, ed. Thomas A. Knott and David C. Fowler (Baltimore, 1952), p. 170.

over-all meaning for each term and expects the reader to perceive it, such treatment of the terms is puzzling.

A preliminary glance at the A-text will illustrate the point. Dobest here seems to have troubled the poet. In only two A-text passages does he define Dobest clearly, and the second was apparently unsatisfactory, for he changed it in B. In A, Thought tells the Dreamer that Dobest is above both Dowel and Dobet and bears a bishop's cross.[7] And Clergy gives the term the same meaning: Dobest is a bishop's peer, prince over God's people.[8] Elsewhere in A, Dobest is omitted from the triad [9] or used obscurely: Dowel is to dread, Dobet to suffer, and Dobest arises out of them.[1] Dobest occurs elsewhere in A only in passages where all three terms are used but not explained. Not much is learned about Dobest in A.

The B-text is much more successful in explaining Dobest. Nevertheless, statements about the terms are changed from A, a phenomenon indicating an unstable relationship between the terms and their meanings. Wit's A-text definition of Dowel as dread and of Dobet as suffrance (Dobest was not defined) is revised in B. Dowel is again to fear God, Dobet is changed to fearing God because of love, and Dobest is not to waste time or words.[2] The C-text revises the passage again. Now Dowel is not to waste time or speech or wealth, Dobet is to love our enemies, and Dobest is to convert all lands to Christianity.[3] If Dowel and Dobest are distinct ways of life, it is strange that a value given to Dobest in one version can be transferred to Dowel in another.

In other passages in B the triad is used without communicating any specific meaning for each of the terms. It is used once as a means of decoration, to develop the conventional comparison of the body to a medieval castle, without giving the terms any meaning except that Dowel, Dobet, and Dobest serve the soul.[4] Dame Study berates the Dreamer for desiring to know the difference between Dowel and Dobet and says that unless he lives the life of Dowel, Dobet will he never, though Dobest draw on him every day. He has learned nothing about the meaning of the terms, though he is being told not to try to learn the most advanced lessons before mastering and practicing humbler teachings. She also advises him to "love lelly" if Dowel is his liking, for Dobet and Dobest are of love's kin.[5] Clergy says Piers Plowman teaches

7. A.ix.86.
8. A.xi.194–5.
9. Dobest is omitted at A.x.11–13 (cf. B.ix.14, C.xi.140) and at A.x.76–99 (cf. B.ix.96–103).
1. A.x.114–23, 211–13.
2. B.ix.94–7.
3. C.xi.182–92.
4. ix.1–16. For a possible explanation of Dowel, Dobet, and Dobest in this passage see below, p. 51.
5. x.130–4; 187–8.

that Dowel and Dobet are two infinites, which, with a faith, find out Dobest, which shall save man's soul—an explanation too obscure for Conscience to understand.[6]

The instability of relationship between terms and meanings is further illustrated by the fact that meanings assigned to one term will elsewhere be assigned to another. Love is Dowel according to Dame Study and Imaginatif, it is Dobet according to Wit, and it is Dobest according to Patience.[7] To practice what you preach is Dobet according to Clergy, but it is Dobest according to the learned Doctor.[8] To help all men is Dobet, says Thought, but it is Dobest according to Wit.[9] Coghill has noticed this phenomenon and has commented on it:

> It will be quickly noticed that the virtues of Dowel encroach upon those of Dobet, and Dobest, as though at first Langland had not completely disentangled the virtues proper to it from those proper to the other two. Nor is this apparent confusion surprising, for he is emphatic that whoever would Dobet, must first Dowel; so also with Dobest. Thus, much of what belongs to Dobet and Dobest also belongs to Dowel, and all that belongs to Dowel, belongs also to Dobet and Dobest. For the Lives are Infinites, can be lived inexhaustibly without contradiction among themselves.[1]

The weakness of this explanation is its subtlety. No reader could be expected to keep all the statements about each term together in his mind, add them up to get a grand total for each, and then notice that some statements are given for more than one term. Yet Coghill has part of the poet's meaning dependent on just such involved analysis. The "apparent confusion" suggests, I submit, that the poet did not disentangle the virtues proper to Dowel from those proper to Dobet and Dobest because he did not conceive of Dowel, Dobet, and Dobest as separate entities. The unstable relationship between the terms and their meanings is understandable if Dobet and Dobest have no separate value, if always they are giving instruction about one and the same way of life, Dowel, the good life.

There are also a number of instances in which one or two terms are omitted from the triad with no observable significance in the omission. Dowel and Dobet are referred to and Dobest is omitted on five occasions;[2] Dowel is mentioned and Dobet and Dobest are omitted on four.[3] Some of the omissions prove my point with special force. When

6. XIII.119–29.
7. Dame Study: x.187; Imaginatif: XII.30; Wit: IX.200: Patience: XIII.138.
8. Clergy: x.251–5; Doctor: XIII.117.
9. Thought: VIII.86; Wit: IX.202.
1. *MedAev*, 2, 128–9.
2. X.129–31, 331, 373; XI.47, 50.
3. X.213, 330–1; XI.402; XIII.220.

the Dreamer complains to Scripture that "Where Dowel is, or Dobet ·
derkelich ȝe shewen," [4] there is surely no implication that Dobest is,
on the contrary, quite clear. When he says he now knows what Dowel is
—to see much and suffer more [5]—the reader can hardly assume that
he does not know Dobet or Dobest. Such a point would have to be
made explicitly. Yet no explanation of Dobet and Dobest is given, and
so what are they? When Conscience and Patience talk of Dowel, [6]
the fact that they do not talk of Dobet and Dobest can hardly mean
they deliberately refrained from talking about these "ways of life."
These omissions are understandable if Dobet and Dobest are merely
convenient divisions of Dowel which can be omitted when the alliteration does not demand them, where to include them would make a line
too long, or where the poet has no particular meanings or divisions
of thought to assign them. Dowel, however, is *never* omitted. There
is never a reference to Dobet or Dobest alone. If they are distinct ways
of life, it is odd the poet never had occasion to discuss them separately
in the course of *Dowel* (which, according to Coghill, contains the moral
argument of the whole poem).

Finally, there are a number of instances in which Dowel is used as
though it were a synonym for the triad. A question about Dowel alone
will evoke a reply about all three terms, [7] or a question about Dowel,
Dobet, and Dobest will be answered with an explanation of Dowel
alone. [8] Consider the following passage:

> And Dowel is to drede god · and Dobet to suffre,
> And so cometh Dobest of bothe · and bryngeth adoun the mody,
> And that is wikked Wille · that many werke shendeth,
> And dryueth away Dowel · thorugh dedliche synnes. [9]

In the last line "Dowel" appears to refer, not to one particular kind of
life or action, but to the good life. That is, the poet is not saying that
wicked will destroys Dowel, "to drede god," but doesn't destroy Dobet,
"to suffre," or Dobest. Dowel is used generically and covers all three
terms. Again, the Dreamer asks Imaginatif what Dowel, Dobet, and
Dobest are. Imaginatif replies that Paul tells what Dowel is—faith,
hope, and charity, and charity is best: "For he doth wel with-oute
doute · that doth as lewte techeth. . . ." [1] Here Dowel, as used by Imaginatif, must be synonymous with all three terms. His speech is an answer
to the Dreamer's question. To ssume Imaginatif is deliberately avoid-

4. X.373.
5. XI.399–402.
6. XIII.220.
7. VIII.78–9, X.217–29, XIII.118–28. Cf. XIII.114–17.
8. VIII.123–IX.1; IX.203–6; XII.26–33; XIII.97–102, 136–52.
9. IX.203–6.
1. XII.33.

ing any reference to Dobet and Dobest is to impute an impossible subtlety to the passage.

This fluid use of the triad suggests that the poet did not have a fixed value for each term. And this fluidity, combined with the fact that he never discusses Dobet and Dobest individually, and the contrast between the first and last appearances of Dowel and those of the triad all suggest that the triad is a literary device, a comparison of the term Dowel which enables the poet to give twofold or threefold answers about the good life when necessary. But the triad always has the basic, literal meaning of Dowel, i.e. "do good," "lead the good life that wins salvation." [2]

This explanation makes understandable another curious phenomenon, the complete absence of the terms from *Dobet* and *Dobest*. If there is some relationship between the definitions of Dobet and the *Dobet* section, it makes no sense for the term Dobet never to appear there. But

---

2. There is evidence outside the text which supports this thesis. Several documents contemporary with *Piers Plowman* and associated with the poem employ the terms Dowel, Dobet, and Dobest and use them in their literal sense. John Ball's famous letter to the commons of Essex, which refers to Piers the Plowman, contains the line "and do welle and bettre, and fleth synne" (Thomas Walsingham, *Historia Anglicana*, ed. Henry Thomas Riley, Rolls Series, London, 1863–64, *2*, 34). Burdach, *Ackermann*, pp. 171–203, contends that Ball's letter is a direct echo of *Piers Plowman*. The letter quoted in the *Chronicon Henrici Knighton*, ed. J. R. Lumby, Rolls Series (London, 1889–95), *2*, 139, reads: "Jakke Carter prayes ȝowe alle that ȝe make a gode ende of that ȝe hane begunnen, and doþ wele and ay bettur and bettur, for at the even men heryth the day." Dowel and Dobet here certainly do not mean the active and contemplative lives or any ways of life. They are used as an exhortation to intensify effort in an activity thought of as good (Dowel). The terms also appear in *Mum and the Sothsegger*, a poem closely associated with *Piers Plowman*, though not, as Skeat suggested, by the same author. See *Mum and the Sothsegger*, ed. Mabel Day and Robert Steele, EETS, o.s. *199* (London, 1936), ix, xiv, xv–xviii. All three terms appear, and they are used in their literal sense. Some members of Parliament, the poet says, "dradde dukis and Do-well for-soke" (iv.93). Mum is called a bad servant for not revealing the truth: such a servant " 'Mote dwelle with þe deueil til Do Bette hym helpe.' " (Section M, 276) Here "Do Bette" is used literally; it means "doing better," "improving," "changing his ways for the better." The monks refuse admittance to the poet because he is poor, though they were founded to care for the poor: "yit faillen þay ofte That þay doon not eche day do beste of alle" (M, 542–3). The speaker says to Mum, who has asserted that churchmen should tell rulers the truth, " 'And yf þou woldes do wel wende to þaym alle And telle þe same tale þat þou has tolde here. . . .' " (M, 772–3). The beekeeper, describing how Lucifer traps man with sin, says covetousness clings to man's heart, " 'Or elles dreede forto do wel dulleth his wittz' " (M, 1170). And, asserting that the Truth-teller dwells in man's heart, he warns that man must beware, for Mum's servant, " 'Antecrist-is angel þat eche day vs ennoyeth,' " tries to gain entry by wiles into Truth-teller's house and debates each day "with Do-welle withynne; ' " when he gains the upper hand, ' "Thenne dreede with a dore-barre dryueth oute þe beste, And maketh þe sothe-sigger seche a newe place' " (M, 1254 ff.). These passages, though not offered as crucial evidence, do tend to support my explanation of the terms Dowel, Dobet, and Dobest. Howard Meroney has some examples of the triad in Latin and one in English: "The Life and Death of Longe Wille," *ELH*, *17* (1950), 15–17.

there is no discussion of Dobet in *Dobet,* no use of the term. The same is true of *Dobest,* except for the passage in which Christ's life and teachings are divided into three parts, labeled Dowel, Dobet, and Dobest.[3] It seems to be *Hamlet* without the Prince of Denmark. On the other hand, if the triad is a device which serves the poet's purpose in *Dowel* alone, its absence from the remainder of the poem is understandable. *Dowel* centers on man's intellectual soul and its capacity for informing man about the nature of the good life (Dowel) and for guiding him in his efforts to pursue the good life. It is the nature of the intellectual soul to ask questions, to make distinctions, and to acquire various kinds of knowledge. The triad Dowel, Dobet, and Dobest is the device by which the poet shows these activities of the intellectual soul while at the same time giving his reader a great deal of moral advice, all of it centering on Dowel, the good life lived in obedience to the law of love. When the quest for information about the good life has ended, when the poet has finished with the intellectual soul, he drops the triad. When he uses it once again in *Dobest,* it is a device once more, a way of making a division in Christ's life and teachings. But since Dobet and Dobest are not terms for specific ways of life, and *Dobet* and *Dobest* do not show ways of life, there is no need for the terms to appear in these sections.

This explanation of the terms leads also, I believe, to an explanation of the titles. I have argued that there is no correlation of meaning between the *Dobet* section and what is said about Dobet in *Dowel,* or between *Dobest* and what is said about Dobest. There is, however, a basic similarity in function and meaning between the terms and the section titles. The triad is a device for labeling divisions—divisions in activities, in kinds of moral effort, in processes like that of penance, etc. The section titles are likewise a device for labeling the divisions of the second part of the poem. And the terms describe one way of life, are used in their literal sense, and represent degrees of comparison— well, better, best. The same is true of the titles. All three sections, *Dowel, Dobet,* and *Dobest,* are devoted to one way of life, the good life of obedience to the law of love, the life which will win salvation. The section titles are also to be read literally. They, too, are degrees of comparison. What is shown in *Dowel* reveals how man can do well. What is shown in *Dobet* reveals how man can do better; it reveals the aids and teachings which enable man to live the good life more successfully and with greater hope of salvation. And what is shown in *Dobest* reveals how man can do best of all. I think this is the meaning of the titles. Part of their mystery is their simplicity. And part of it is the confusion created by the poet's use of Dowel, Dobet, and Dobest in

3. XIX.104–83.

the text of *Dowel* and as titles for divisions of his poem. He was, however, using the triad in both circumstances with essentially the same meaning and for essentially the same function. For all the confusion, the text and the titles lead finally to this simple answer: By Dowel, Dobet, and Dobest the third he meant, in text and title, do well, do better, do best—nothing more.

5

The Visions of Dowel

PIERS' pardon has commanded man to do well if he would be
saved. In the visions of *Dowel,* the Dreamer begins his search
for Dowel—that is, he seeks a knowledge of what is involved
in the process of doing well, the rules and modes of right action.
Basically, Dowel is to obey the law of love, the primary principle which
Holy Church taught the Dreamer early in the *Visio.* Indeed, this same
law is the basic doctrine of the *Dobet* and *Dobest* visions also. But Holy
Church's simple pronouncement of the law of love has left much unsaid
and unexplained. A complex structure of dogma and ethical doctrine
had been built on that law as a foundation. Some of that dogma and
doctrine will be expounded in *Dowel, Dobet, and Dobest.* The poem
is, of course, no mere vade mecum of orthodox morality. The poet
makes a personal selection of doctrines, and although he may evade
heresy, he is not in mad pursuit of pure orthodoxy. In particular, he
follows his own vision in making his matter focus so sharply on the
law of love. Just as much the poet's own creation is his explanation of
what Holy Church left largely unexplained, *how* man can obey the law
of love. As I have said, he sees mankind enabled to obey this law and
be saved by virtue of a plan, a scheme of salvation in which each Person
of the Trinity participates to assist mankind to obey the law in greater
and greater degree so that ultimately it can be saved.

In his quest to learn the what and the how of doing good, the
Dreamer becomes involved in the drama of man's intellectual soul. For
he is in search of knowledge, and such a search demands first of all
the application of man's intellectual powers. His intellectual soul, moreover, is the first source of man's moral power. It is the gift of God the
Father, and it is by this gift that God created man in His image: "Non
ergo secundum corpus, sed secundum intellectum mentis ad imaginem
dei creatus est homo." [1] Because he has a rational soul man is able to
know the good, conform to it, and win salvation:

---

1. Bede, *Hexaemeron,* PL, *91,* col. 29. A medieval writer rarely refers to the
creation of man without making this point. Cf. Peter Comestor, *Historia Scholastica,*
PL, *198,* col. 1063, and St. Thomas Aquinas, *Summa Theologica,* I, q. 93, where various writers are cited.

by his owne kynde it [the soul] may kindely deme. . . . And
kindly it desireth good and fleeth euyll / though it chose euylle
otherwhyle by defaute of auysement: but by kind it forsaketh
euyll, and grutcheth therayenst / as saint Aust. saith. So the soule
vegetatiue desireth to be, the sensible desireth to be well, & the
reasonable soule desireth to be best. And therfore it resteth neuer,
tyll it be ioyned with the best. For the place of the reasonable
soule is god, to whom ward it is meued that it may rest in him.
And this meuyng is not by changynge of place, but rather by loue
and desire.[2]

This is the answer to the question of how man can know what is
good and how he can do good. For this reason the intellectual soul is
the subject of the narrative in *Dowel*. Faculties of the intellectual soul
appear as characters, as do objects or products of the soul's activity,
like Clergy (learning) and Scripture (writing). The intellectual soul's
capacity for knowing and doing good is examined, and at the same
time the course of right action perceived by the soul is revealed. The
first vision of *Dowel* examines the soul's (i.e. man's) powers to *know*
the good; the second vision examines man's ability to *do* what he knows
to be good. The course of right action is suggested in the first vision
and preached in considerable detail in the second.

The inherent desire of the soul for the good is also used to motivate

2. Bartholomaeus Anglicus, *De Proprietatibus Rerum* (London, 1535), Bk. III, chap.
xiii (John Trevisa's translation). One must turn to either the scholastics or the
encyclopedists as the probable sources of the poet's knowledge of psychology. Both
followed a traditional description of the soul based ultimately on Aristotle. Compare,
for example, the account of the soul in the "Treatise on Man" in the *Summa Theologica*,
I, qq. 75–87, with that in Bartholomaeus Anglicus, Bk. III. The scholastics, however,
worked out elaborate descriptions of the soul and argued over specific details. The
encyclopedists transmitted, without debate, a somewhat incoherent description arrived
at by a not very discriminating eclecticism. Father Dunning, Greta Hort, and Robertson and Huppé make use of scholastic sources in interpreting the "psychology" in the
poem. Greta Hort goes so far as to assign the poet to a particular school of scholastic
psychology, the Victorine-Thomistic school: *Piers Plowman and Contemporary
Thought* (London, n.d.), pp. 65–7, 84–5. Because the encyclopedists were more accessi-
ble sources of knowledge, however, and because the poet quotes a description of the
soul that goes back to the encyclopedist Isidore of Seville and that was repeated by
other encyclopedists, I shall use them rather than the scholastics in explaining the
poet's terms. Mensendieck, the first to show the poet had a knowledge of psychology,
turned to the encyclopedists Bartholomaeus Anglicus and Vincent de Beauvais to explain the poet's terms: "Die Verfasserschaft der drei Texte des Piers the Plowman,"
ZVgL, new ser. *18* (1910), 25–7.
The poet's description of the soul is given in Latin at B.xv.39, in translation at
xv.23–36. This description first appeared in Isidore's *Etymologiarum Libri XX*, Bk.
XI, chap. i, PL *82*, col. 399, and, in slightly different form, in his *Differentiarum,
sive de proprietate sermonum, Libri Duo*, Bk. II, chap. xxix, PL *83*, col. 84. It appears
also in Alcuin's *De Animae Ratione Liber ad Eulalium Virginem*, PL *101*, col. 644, and
in Bartholomaeus Anglicus, Bk. III, chap. v.

the narrative in the first vision of *Dowel*. Again and again the Dreamer expresses a desire to have a "kynde knowing,"[3] a natural knowledge, of Dowel. After the friar has expounded his parable, the Dreamer sighs that he has "no kynde knowyng" to understand his words but hopes to learn better.[4] The first vision follows immediately. To Thought's explanation of Dowel, Dobet, and Dobest he replies that he does not understand and desires "more kuynde knowynge."[5] So they seek out Wit. Later he asks Dame Study to teach him "kyndely to knowe what is Dowel."[6] After telling him the sciences she has created, Dame Study bids him ask Clergy and Scripture to teach him "kyndely to knowe what is Dowel."[7] And he does. The phrase is not used during the second vision of *Dowel*, where the issue is not knowledge but practice. But when the vision has ended, the Dreamer says it was long before he could "kyndely knowe what was Dowel."[8] Then the Soul appears and tells the Dreamer the soul's many names and functions, but accuses him of wanting to master all knowledge. The Dreamer confesses his desire to know all sciences and crafts "kyndely" in his heart.[9] The Soul rebukes him but tells him the nature of charity. With the explanation of charity the quest is apparently ended, for there are no more questions about Dowel and no more requests for a "kynde knowing."[1]

3. The phrase is first used in the scene with Holy Church: I.136–7, 140–2, 161–3.

4. VIII.57–8.

5. B.VIII.108 is obviously a fusion of two lines. The alliteration is faulty, and A and C agree against B. Cf. A.IX. 102–3 and C.XI.107–8. The A-text reads: " 'But зit sauereth not me thi siggynge . so me God helpe, More kuynde knowynge . I coueyte to here. . . .' "

6. X.146.

7. X.216–17.

8. XV.1–2.

9. XV.48–9.

1. Father Dunning discusses the meaning of "kynde knowing" but not its narrative function in *Dowel*. He considers it identical in meaning with "kynde wit": *Piers Plowman*, p. 39. Cf. also Greta Hort, p. 69, and Randolph Quirk, "Langland's Use of *Kind Wit* and *Inwit*," *JEGP, 52* (1953), 184. Father Dunning, however, believes "kynde wit" and "kynde knowing" mean "conscience" or "synderesis": pp. 36–9, 50–1. But the fact that in A, B, and C the poet uses the terms "conscience" and "reason" and makes Conscience and Reason characters in his poem suggests that there is a distinction in meaning between those terms and "kynde wit" and "kynde knowing." Moreover, in *Dowel* (B-text) the poet shows that "kynde wit" must be kept under careful control; he does not think of "kynde wit" as a purely moral faculty. Greta Hort (pp. 69–72) identifies "kynde wit" and "kynde knowing" with the scholastic *lex naturalis*. But her argument rests on the untenable assumption that the personification "Kynde Wit" is an allegorical character and therefore really stands for something else, namely, *lex naturalis*. The most careful investigation of the meaning of the terms is that of Quirk. He finds that the poet's "kind wit" corresponds to Reginald Pecock's "natural logic," which is common to beasts and unlearned men; cf. Reginald Pecock, *The Folewer to the Donet*, ed. Elsie Vaughan Hitchcock, EETS, o.s. *164* (London, 1924), 37 ff. The poet uses "kind" not to mean "mortal" or "human" wit but to mean it is natural and in-born in creatures. "Kynde wit" is closely connected with the bodily senses (B. XII.130), whereas reason is capable of comprehending all things imaginable and sensible

It has served its purpose in the narrative. The moral questing of his intellectual soul has led the Dreamer finally to a knowledge of goodness: the law of love.

The drama of *Dowel* is the drama of the intellectual soul in action, its strength and its weakness, its errors and its triumphs. In the first vision of *Dowel* doubts about the real value of the intellectual soul cause the major crisis in the action. The Dreamer's suspicions of intelligence are the suspicions of an age of faith skeptical of reason. These suspicions were toughened apparently by the poet's own observation of intellectual arrogance and failures of conduct among the friars and the learned and his own sympathy for the simple piety of the ignorant plowman. But if the Dreamer's mistakes and presumptions reveal the fallibility of human intelligence, his final victory is evidence of the soul's power. His balanced assessment of the limitations and virtues of the intelligence, and the knowledge of patient poverty to which he ultimately attains, are a vindication of the intellectual soul.

In the interlude in the real world before the first vision of *Dowel* begins,[2] the Dreamer seeks to discover where Dowel dwells. Two Minorite friars assert that Dowel dwells with them, and one of the friars tells the Dreamer a parable to prove it. The Dreamer, however, understands neither the parable nor its explanation. He falls asleep, and the first dream of *Dowel* begins.

It is unsatisfactory to dismiss the scene with the friars as irrelevant satire.[3] The tone of much of the scene is serious. There are incidental flashes of irony, and no one is expected to believe the friars' claim to be the home of Dowel. On the whole, however, they are treated respectfully. The Dreamer does not make a direct attack on friars, he states a general proposition: all men sin, even the best. And the friar answers in general terms, with no special pleading for his order. Why, then, were the Minorites introduced if not for satire? The Franciscans had a formidable reputation for learning in England in the fourteenth

---

without recourse to the imagination or the senses. Quirk concludes that in *Piers Plowman* the two terms "wit" and "kynde wit" are an attempt to represent the unity of and at the same time the distinction between the *vis cogitativa* (corresponding to the *vis aestimativa* in animals) and the *ratio particularis*: Quirk, 182–5.

2. VIII.1–69.

3. As, e.g., Carnegy, p. 19; Wells, "Construction," 136–7; Chambers, *Mind.* p. 125. The friar's analogy is so mixed up that "it means nothing," says Stone, "An Interpretation of the A-Text," *PMLA, 53*, 667. But the revision of this passage in the C-text (C.XI.33–55), which alters somewhat the teaching of the sermon and its emphasis of some points, can be explained only if the ideas of the sermon were of some concern to the poet. Robertson and Huppé, *Scriptural Tradition*, pp. 102–4, consider the scene a serious one but think its main purpose is to show the friars as teachers of false doctrine and the Dreamer as not yet able to distinguish between false spiritual guides and Piers Plowman, the true spiritual guide.

century, and it is their intellect and learning that are stressed.[4] The vision to follow will examine the relation between man's learning and intelligence and his morality. The learned friars and the scholastic controversy with them are an admirable preparation for this theme. So is the sermon of the friar. It cannot be ironic, for it expounds important, orthodox doctrine, nor is it so difficult or confused that "it means nothing." First, Dowel is defined: it is charity. This definition provides the reader with the key meaning of the term for the later discussions of Dowel. Second, the passage states that Dowel is a power possessed by all men. The Dreamer had asked, *"Where* is Dowel?" The friars, by claiming he dwells among them, actually say that Dowel dwells in man. The Dreamer, in observing that even the just man sins, implies that Dowel is impossible for man. By his analogy the friar argues that man, weak and sinful though he be, yet possesses the power to do good. He sins because he has free wit and free will (i.e. an intellectual soul), but free wit and free will are also the source of his ability to do well. The analogy announces the theme of the first vision of *Dowel:* the powers and limitations for moral action of man's God-given rational soul. The Dreamer's doubts about man's ability to do well are a preparation for his later skepticism. The friars themselves adumbrate a major dilemma in the vision. There has been sufficient abuse of friars in the *Visio* for the reader to assume these friars are probably not good men. Yet they have a glib and accurate knowledge of the nature of goodness. Of what worth is such knowledge, the Dreamer will later ask bitterly, if its fruits are not good deeds? Far from being a digression, the interlude introduces the main ideas of the first vision.

In his dream the first character the Dreamer meets is Thought, by which is meant the process of knowing or the power by which man knows, i.e. mind.[5] Thought's statement that he has followed the Dreamer for seven years, if not meaningless,[6] refers to the beginning of

4. Cf. Mensendieck, "The Authorship of Piers Plowman," *JEGP, 9* (1910), 406. On the distinguished school of the Franciscans in London in the fourteenth century see C. L. Kingsford, *The Grey Friars of London,* British Society of Franciscan Studies, 6 (Aberdeen, 1915), 21 f.

5. Cf. B.xv.39, "dum scit, Mens est," translated in B " 'And for that I can and knowe called am I *Mens'* " (xv.25), but translated in C as " 'mannys Thouht' " (C.xvii.185). Cf. *OED,* "thought," sb.I., 1.b: "As a function or attribute of a living being; the capacity of thinking; the thinking faculty; in early use often nearly mind." This seems closer to the poet's meaning than Greta Hort's explanation of "Thought" as the scholastic *intellectus agens,* the link between the knowledge of universal ideas which a man possesses and the concrete instances he observes: p. 89. To Robertson and Huppé (p. 104), "Thought represents those ideas concerning the way to achieve Truth of which Will is at the moment capable."

6. viii.75. Cf. Fritz Krog, "Autobiographische oder Typische Zahlen in *Piers Plowman?" Anglia, 58* (1934), 319–23. Krog argues that the number seven here is merely

intellectual activity and of moral responsibility at the age of seven [7]—
"post septem annos sunt doli capaces" is the canonist's phrase.[8]

Thought teaches what man's mind tells him about the good life when
he first reflects upon the problem. Higher intellectual faculties will
have more important counsels to give him later in the poem. It is
Thought who introduces the triad of Dowel, Dobet, and Dobest: Dowel
guides himself by the rule of righteousness, Dobet helps others, and
Dobest bears a bishop's crown. All three have appointed one to be king
and rule by their three wits.[9] This may be a description of the Three
Ways of Life, as many have maintained. If so, it is a rather mechanical
and superficial description, not the product of higher intellectual faculties, and the Dreamer rejects it as not to his liking.[1] He wants "a
more kynde knowyng." If this is a recommendation of the Three Lives,
it is the clearest recommendation in the poem. It is not sufficient evidence, however, to argue that the Three Lives are the poet's Dowel,
Dobet, and Dobest.

The quest now turns to Wit. Thought without information from
the senses cannot be very illuminating. Wit quite clearly is the senses.
The Latin *sensus* ("Dum sentit, sensus est") is later translated as
"wit": "And whan I fele that folke telleth · my firste name is *Sensus,
And that is wytte and wisdome · the welle of alle craftes.*" [2] Wit is the

---

conventional, not autobiographical, as Allen Bright contended: *New Light on "Piers
Plowman"* (London, 1928), p. 54. The autobiographical interpretation reads too much
into the number. Burdach, in rejecting Mensendieck's autobiographical thesis for
Dowel, remarks that the Middle Ages were not autobiographical and that autobiography would be alien to the spirit of social and religious reform in the poem, however
much the poet might have used particular experiences in individual passages: *Ackermann,* p. 326, n. 1. Krog's interpretation of the number as merely conventional, however, is not the only other possible explanation. See below.

7. Cf. Bede Jarrett, *Social Theories of the Middle Ages* (London, 1926), p. 34. After
his seventh year a child had to know his Pater Noster, Ave Maria, and Creed: *Sermons,*
p. 12. Mensendieck, referring to A.IX.109 ff., 113 ff., calls the meeting of Thought
and Wit a naive but expressive picture of awakening understanding, and the ranking
of the bishop as Dobest "Kinderträume": *Charakterentwickelung,* pp. 12, 29.

8. William Lyndwood, *Provinciale (seu Constitutiones Angliae . . .)* (Oxford,
1679), p. 202.

9. VIII.78–106.

1. VIII.108.

2. XV.29–30. Cf. Bartholomaeus Anglicus, Bk. III, chap. vi, where "wytte" is defined
as "the vertue of the soule, wherby she knoweth thynges sensible and corporall, whan
they ben present." This meaning of "wit" is also established by H. S. V. Jones, "Imaginatif in Piers Plowman," *JEGP, 13* (1914), 583–4, and n. 1, 583. Randolph Quirk observes that the word "wit" had a great range of meaning in ME and that this same
range of meaning for the term is to be found in *Piers Plowman.* The term is applied
to any mental or sensual faculty, the "outer" senses, as in B.XIV.54; to a special skill or
art, as in B.XIX.118; it is grouped broadly with "wisdom," as in B.XV.30; it can mean
acumen, ranging from base cunning, as in C.VII.258, to the wisdom which leads to philo-
sophic thought, as in B.IX, *passim* (i.e. the character Wit which I am defining here):
"*Kind Wit and Inwit,*" *JEGP, 52* (1953), 182. While not denying the range of meaning which the term possesses in Middle English and in the poem, I would still argue

great source of knowledge, for through his senses man learns about the world around him, and through his senses he can come to know certain basic moral laws. The value for salvation of what man can learn by wit will be one of the principal issues debated in *Dowel*.

In the long, rambling speech of Wit is contained some of the knowledge that the senses can bring to man—an analysis of man's body and of man's soul, of inwit as the protector of the soul, of Kynde (God as creator of the world and of man), and of marriage, not to mention sundry warnings and pieces of good counsel.[3] The main point of Wit's speech is clear. Since the Dreamer met the friars, the question in his mind has been, can man do well? This was the question he was asking when he inquired where Dowel, Dobet, and Dobest were and whether Dowel was a man. Wit replies that Dowel dwells in man, for man has been given a soul (Anima) by Kynde. Kynde protects the soul against Satan by several means, but especially by inwit. The implication is that man is capable of doing well.

Some of the details of the speech, however, are obscure. The roles which Wit assigns to Dowel, Dobet, and Dobest as aides of Anima [4] are puzzling. They are not the Three Ways of Life, but three powers within the body that protect the soul. Are they St. Augustine's will, understanding, and memory, an image of the Trinity in man? [5] Are they the vegetable, animal or sensible, and rational souls? [6] Or the concupiscible, irascible, and reasonable souls? [7] No certain answer seems possible. But whatever the triad represents, the passage does unquestionably assert that man can protect his soul and do well.

What is the meaning of inwit? The word meant both conscience, inward sense of right and wrong; and reason, intellect, understanding, wisdom. In the plural, "inwits" meant the five internal intellectual powers, will, reason, mind, imagination, and thought.[8] Though something of the first sense, "conscience," may have been in the poet's mind when he used the word,[9] the primary sense which "inwit" had for him

---

that the explanation of wit which I have suggested best fits the context here, where Wit is a personification and presumably a faculty of the soul, the faculty *sensus* in the definition of the soul at B.xv.29–30.

3. IX.1–106.

4. IX.1–16.

5. St. Augustine, *On the Trinity* [De Trinitate], *Libri XV*, trans. Arthur West Haddan and William G. T. Shedd, NP-N, *3*, 142–3 (Bk. X, chaps. 11–12). Cf. Isidore, *Etymologiarum*, Bk. VII, chap. iv, PL, *82*, col. 271; Alcuin, *De Animae Ratione*, PL, *101*, col. 641; Aquinas, *Summa Theologica*, I, q. 93, vii; *Cursor Mundi*, EETS, o.s. *57* (London, 1874), *1*, lines 562–8.

6. Bartholomaeus Anglicus, Bk. III, chap. xiii.

7. Alcuin, *De Animae Ratione*, PL, *101*, cols. 639–41; Bartholomaeus Anglicus, Bk. III, chap. vi.

8. OED, "inwit."

9. Skeat interpreted "inwit" here as "conscience": *Parallel Texts*, *2*, 139; Father Dunning as "reason": *Piers Plowman*, p. 174; Greta Hort as *sensus communis*: *Con-*

was probably "intellect." When he meant "conscience" he used the word "conscience." Here, talking of Kynde's creation of the soul, he would probably be thinking of the rational power of the soul, which the commentators on Genesis i: 27 stressed.[1] The poet is saying that inwit, the intellect, enables man to protect his soul and do good. A contemporary wrote of the "inwits": "These be þe wittys þe whiche God has geuen us to knowe hym wiþ, and to rewle us thorwȝ wysdam, and leve [lyue] holy lyf, as good servauntys of God schuld do, and eschewe perelys of synne, and for to come to þat joye þat God has ordeynyd us to be made fore." [2] This is essentially the value ascribed to "inwit" in Wit's speech.

Finally, the definitions of Dowel, Dobet, and Dobest that conclude the discussion of inwit [3] seem unrelated to what has gone before. (Dowel is the fear of God, Dobet is the fear of God because of love,

---

temporary Thought, pp. 94–7. In his translation Henry Wells renders "inwit" as "conscience," "True judgment," and "Judgment" (IX.17, 50, 54). Coghill calls it "Conscience": *The Pardon*, p. 24. "Inwit" clearly means "intellect" at A.x.71–4: contrasted with those who lack inwit are those of "wys vnderstondinge." The talk about conscience at A.x.87–92, however, suggests that the poet was not distinguishing sharply between the sense of "intellect" and the sense of "conscience" when he used "inwit" in this passage. The reference to conscience is omitted in B and C. This view of "inwit," which I arrived at independently, is largely supported by Randolph Quirk in his careful investigation of the term. He points out that the distinction between the soul and the highest mental faculty, intellect, was never satisfactorily established by the scholastic philosophers, and so we find "inwit" recorded in practically all the senses of the Latin *animus;* for the most part, however, it signifies, more or less vaguely, the human faculty of comprehension. "Langland's usage," he says, "is precise and technical to a degree hard to parallel in ME; *inwit* is 'intellect,' the *agens* aspect of *intellectus* in Thomist terms, and since the intellect is concerned with the apprehension of truth, it is therefore concerned with the distinction between true and false, good and evil; hence its functions can come near to, and be confused with, those of conscience." And he observes, "Langland is not one of the ME writers who use 'inwit' for 'conscience'; he maintains a consistent and scholastically accurate distinction between the two concepts. . . . This is not to say that he makes 'conscience' a separate faculty from 'inwit'; conscience is rather one aspect of inwit's activity; it is inwit's awareness of right and wrong brought to bear upon one's actions; it is inwit in action." *JEGP, 52,* 185–8.

1. Genesis i: 27 clearly lies behind this passage on inwit. The word "Faciamus" at B.IX.35 proves this. There are, in fact, reminiscences of Genesis throughout Wit's speech. Cf. the references to Adam and Eve (IX.33–4), to Cain (120–2), to Seth (123–9) and to Noah (130–43). God in the speech is God the Creator, the God of Genesis, "Kynde," " 'a creatour of alle kynnes thinges; Fader and fourmour of al that euere was maked' " (26–7).

2. *Select Wycliff, 3,* 118.

3. B.IX.92–106. Dowel is to dread God. The Scriptures are the source for this doctrine, as his quotation shows: Psalms cx: 10 (Vulgate), Ecclesiasticus i: 16. A number of passages in ME which echo the doctrine are noted by Sister Mary Frances Smith in *Wisdom and Personification of Wisdom Occurring in Middle English Literature before 1500* (Washington, D.C., 1935), pp. 43–6, 55. It was a favorite dictum of the moralists. Cf. *Vices and Virtues,* p. 118; *Speculum Christiani,* p. 48. Dobet, to fear God out of love rather than out of fear of vengeance, is also found in the moralists: ibid., pp. 38, 218; *Vices and Virtues,* pp. 73–4; *Sermons,* pp. 34–5. Dobest is not to waste time or speech. Wasting time is warned against in Walter Hilton's "On Daily Work" in *Yorkshire Writers, 1,* 136–7, in *Speculum Christiani,* pp. 88–90, and in *Vices and Virtues,* pp. 14, 42, 49, 55 (which also warns against idle words), 133.

Dobest is wasting neither speech nor time.) They contain good, somewhat conventional moral advice. Perhaps, since man has been shown
to be capable of moral action because he possesses inwit, moral advice
is appropriate here. Perhaps this is the kind of counsel inwit can give
man.

After discussing the soul and inwit, Wit praises marriage [4] and concludes with two sets of apparently irrelevant definitions of Dowel,
Dobet, and Dobest. Actually they constitute an assertion by Wit that
those living in the state of matrimony ordained by God are capable of
the moral action necessary for salvation. Neither set of definitions has
any connection with the Three Ways of Life. The first set says Dowel
is to obey the law, Dobet is to love friend and foe (the law specifically),
and Dobest is to care for young and old, to heal and help (the law of
love spelled out in more detail).[5] The triad recommends a successively
more intense, more specific course of moral action which all men, not
some particular group, should follow. In the second set of definitions
(repeated from A but dropped in C), Dowel is to dread God, Dobet is
to suffer, and Dobest is the power, growing out of the first two actions,
to subdue the wicked will, which destroys many works and drives
away Dowel (i.e. the ability to do good) through deadly sin.[6] This
last appears to mean that the wicked will, i.e. the deliberate commission of sin, destroys charity in the soul and so undoes the value for
salvation of good works (" 'many werke shendeth' "). Wicked will also
makes it impossible for one to do well, inasmuch as while the soul is
without charity because of mortal sin, one cannot do good works, or
good works are of no avail to salvation. In his parable sermon the
friar had taught much the same doctrine.

Wit, a faculty of the intellectual soul, has made a twofold contribution to the Dreamer's understanding of Dowel. His reply to the question about Dowel, Dobet, and Dobest, though it includes a number of
topics, actually concentrates on two points: a description of the soul
and an analysis of the married state. These topics seem an ill-mated
couple, but man's rational soul and the institution of matrimony were
paired in the biblical account of the beginning of human history:

4. IX.107–98.

5. IX.199–202. There is perhaps some special connection between the married state,
which Wit has been discussing, and the law of love, which he recommends here. Those
properly married have been motivated by love, and so the law of love is suggested by,
and realized in, right marriage. Later Imaginatif says charity is best for salvation and
then adds, " 'For he doth wel with-oute doute that doth as lewte techeth; That is, if
thow be man maried, thi make thow louye, And lyue forth as lawe wole while ȝe lyuen
bothe' " (XII.33–5). Here marriage appears to be directly associated with love and the
law.

6. IX.203–6. Sins committed without deliberation are not mortal (*Summa Theologica*,
I–II, q. 74, iii, x), but those committed willfully are mortal (I–II, q. 72, v, and II–II,
q. 13, ii). There can be no true virtue without charity (II–II, q. 23, vii), and it is destroyed by one mortal sin (II–II, q. 24, xii).

Faciamus Hominem ad imaginem, & similitudinem nostram. . . .
Et creauit Deus hominem in imaginem suam : ad imaginem Dei
creauit illum, masculum & feminam creauit eos. Benedixitque illis
Deus, et ait : Crescite et multiplicamini, et replete terram.[7]

The phrase "ad imaginem" is glossed as referring to man's intellectual
soul; [8] and "Crescite," etc., is discussed as proof of the divine institution of marriage.[9] The rational soul and marriage were therefore associated topics in the poet's mind. Wit discusses them because they are
matters knowable by man's wit and are the fundamental prerequisites
for the moral life. Wit's discussion of Dowel, Dobet, and Dobest is
much more penetrating than Thought's description of three kinds of
activity. His discussion of the soul and of marriage shows that God the
Creator, in making man, gave him the capacity to lead a moral life.
He endowed him with a soul, by means of which he can do well and
fight against evil, and established for him the state of matrimony, by
which the weakness of the flesh leads not to sin but to the fulfillment
of God's command to replenish the earth. In addition, some of Wit's
definitions of Dowel, Dobet, and Dobest have given the Dreamer useful moral advice.

Dame Study now enters the dream. She is Wit's wife. This may
mean either that one uses the senses in studying or that study is based
on knowledge derived from the senses. Her first speech[1] develops the
thesis that learning has fallen into disrepute.[2] She also touches on several important topics which will be developed later : the danger of
riches, the necessity of caring for the poor, the importance of doing
what is good rather than merely knowing what is good, and the impiety

7. Genesis i : 26–8.
8. See above, p. 45 and n. 1.
9. Cf. the comments on these verses from Genesis in Bede, *Hexamaeron*, PL, *91*,
cols. 29–31, and in Rabanus Maurus (identical with Bede's), *Commentariorum in
Genesim Libri Quatuor*, I, vii, PL, *107*, cols. 459–61. The two topics are associated in
Peter Comestor's *Historia Scholastica*, PL, *198*, cols. 1063–4 : chap. ix is titled "De
creatione hominis," and chap. x, "De institutione conjugii." Possibly, too, the talk of
marriage is an echo of the Joachimite idea of the first age or dispensation as the age of
the married, the *ordo conjugatorum*, an image of the Father in His fatherly relation.
See above, p. 17, n. 4.
1. x.1–134.
2. The poet's approach to studies and to learning in this speech disregards the conventional association of studies with the university and instead treats studies from the
point of view of the relationship between lord and clerk, and especially lord and minstrel. This fact in itself would refute Mensendieck's view that Dame Study represents
the *studium generale* at the universities : *Charakterentwickelung*, pp. 17–25 ; "The Authorship of Piers Plowman," *JEGP, 9*, 408–14. Equally untenable is his argument that
the subjects Dame Study taught Clergy's wife constitute the trivium and the quadrivium
of the medieval schools. The list (x.171–82) includes such unorthodox items as car-
pentry and masonry. In connection with Dame Study's speech see Donaldson's interesting suggestion that the poet may have been, in his youth at least, a minstrel of sorts—
perhaps a pious minstrel who wrote and spoke on religious subjects (*Piers Plowman*,
pp. 136–53).

of an irreverent seeking after knowledge. This last point has two parts:
she discourages the attempt to distinguish between Dowel and Dobet
as a waste of effort when the real task is to put Dowel into action,[3]
and she warns against trying to know the ways of God instead of having faith and caring for the soul.

In her second speech[4] Dame Study agrees to send the Dreamer to
her cousin Clergy (learning) and his wife, Scripture (writings, especially the Bible). They will teach him to do well. She tells him how
to act if he would become more learned, and lists the fruits of mankind's study, including theology. Theology she condemns as too difficult and too subtle but commends because it teaches man to love. It is
an amusing revelation of the poet's own divided attitude toward learning. She discourses on love at some length and insists that men must
love their enemies. Then at last she sends him on his way. Her speech
has provided one, and only one, definition of Dowel: it is to love. The
Dreamer will not be aware of the importance of this speech for a long
time. The friar in his sermon and Wit at the end of his discourse had
spoken of love, and here it is stressed again. Eventually the Dreamer
will come to see that learning is good if it helps man to know and obey
the law of love. Here Dame Study has told him,

> For-thi loke thow louye · as longe as thow durest,
> For is no science vnder sonne · so souereyne for the soule.[5]

His new mentor, Clergy, tells the Dreamer that Dowel is to believe
what the Church teaches: the articles of faith and especially the doctrine of the Trinity, which cannot be explained but must be believed.
Dobet is to put your belief into action and be what you seem to be.
Then Dobest is possible: you can blame the sinful and try to lead them
back to righteousness. This leads to an attack on men of the church
who are themselves wrong-doers, and on the religious for not following
their rule and helping the poor. If the religious do not reform themselves, some king will reform them, and divide their income with the
friars. And caught up in the prophetic mood, Clergy (speaking for the
poet) threatens that Cain shall come before the reforming king appears,
but Dowel shall destroy him. Although this takes the reader no nearer
to a knowledge of Dowel, it is an interesting glimpse of the complex
of apocalyptic ideas and hopes from which the poem emerged.[6]

---

3. This is the Dreamer's sin in the scenes with Clergy and Scripture, and with Reason. Imaginatif later preaches against this fault in the Dreamer. Dame Study remarks
that Imaginatif will have something to say about irreverent seeking after knowledge:
X.115.

4. X.135–217.

5. X.205–6.

6. X.218–330. Fraternal correction was a duty of all Christians: *Summa Theologica*,
II–II, q. 33; *Speculum Christiani*, pp. 124–6. (I omit from consideration X.291–303, which

Scripture, happily, returns to the subject [7] and contributes to the
Dreamer's moral education by telling him that riches are a hindrance
to salvation. The good life is one of patient poverty.[8] The Gospel teaching that he who is baptized is saved, cited by the Dreamer to prove
the salvation of the rich as well as the poor,[9] applies to heathen baptized *in extremis,* Scripture says. The Christian must do more: he
must obey the command to love God and his neighbor:

> And thus bilongeth to louye · that leueth to be saued.
> And but we do thus in dede · ar the daye of dome,
> It shal bisitten vs ful soure · the siluer that we kepen. . . .[1]

Scripture's reply reveals the relationship in the poet's thought between
riches, patient poverty, and the law of love. Wealth, except under special
conditions, he believes, leads to violation of the law of love; patient
poverty leads to its fulfillment.

And now, suddenly, a crisis appears in the narrative. It appears
none too soon. A series of interviews, though with characters as unusual
as Wit and Clergy, and though in pursuit of the knowledge of good and
evil, quickly palls. The Dreamer unexpectedly challenges Scripture's
statement that moral action is a prerequisite for salvation.[2] He now
believes both morality and learning are worthless. He is skeptical about
the value of moral action because the doctrine of predestination—a
much debated issue of the day—implied that morality was fruitless.
There is no evidence, however, that the poet had read widely in this
controversy, in Bradwardine's *De Causa Dei,*[3] for example, and his
difficulties with predestination have probably been exaggerated.[4] It is a

---

is from R MS.) Nevill Coghill offers an explanation of x.317–30, esp. 321–2, 329–30.
He suggests that the king is Christ and Cain is Antichrist: "Two Notes on *Piers
Plowman," MedAev, 4* (1935), 83–7; *The Pardon,* pp. 42–5. The lines sound to me
more like vague threats of evil forces that will appear but be overcome by man's capacity for good, particularly in the shape of a reforming king. For an example of the
prophetic and apocalyptic writings in the period, see the pieces by the Spiritual Franciscan, John de Pera-Tallada, in *Fasciculus Rerum Expetendarum & Fugiendarum* . . . , ed. Edward Brown (London, 1690), *2,* 494–6, 496–508.

7. x.332–71.

8. The contemporary poem *Patience* may have influenced the poet's belief in patient
poverty. See Robert J. Menner's introduction to *Purity,* Yale Studies in English, *61*
(New Haven, 1920), xxix and n. 2.

9. This line from, apparently, Mark xvi: 16, will be used by the Dreamer in the next
passus to refute the doctrine of predestination (xi.119). In the present scene the line is
used to imply that moral action is irrelevant to salvation, and so it is attacked by Scripture. It will have no such implication in the next passus.

1. x.359–61.

2. x.372–474.

3. x.372–7. For a summary of Thomas Bradwardine's doctrine of predestination see
Howard Rollin Patch, "Troilus on Predestination," *JEGP, 17* (1918), 399–422.

4. Cf. Mensendieck, "The Authorship of Piers Plowman," *JEGP, 9,* 416, who says
the doctrine of predestination "evidently . . . was the stumbling block in the theological
development of our author."

topic, Nevill Coghill aptly remarks, "on which, for a wonder, Langland has less to say than Chaucer." [5] In the following passus he solves
the problem swiftly with two biblical quotations. It serves a narrative
purpose here, however, by helping to create dramatic conflict.

The Dreamer also doubts the value of morality because of the many
evil-doers who have been saved, such as the thief on the cross, and
Mary Magdalene. There are men of learning and good life, he reflects,
but God alone knows whether they or evil men are saved; evil, after
all, enables man to know the good. The truest words God ever spoke,
he concludes bitterly, are "Nemo bonus." [6] The Dreamer attacks learning and intelligence as well as morality. God gave man inwit to protect
his soul by fleeing evil and doing good. Intelligence, therefore, should
help one to win salvation. But the Dreamer is skeptical because he has
been told that learned heathen clerks like Solomon and Aristotle were
not saved.[7] Why, then, pursue learning?

> And if I shulde worke bi here werkes · to wynne me heuene,
> That for her werkes and witte · now wonyeth in pyne,
> Thanne wrouȝte I vnwysely · what-so euere ȝe preche.[8]

He is skeptical, too, because learned clerks do not lead good lives.[9] Of
what good is learning if it does not lead to good deeds? Christ never
commended learning, and there appears to be little respect for learning
in heaven. Indeed, learning seems to be a hindrance to salvation: ignorant plowmen are saved sooner than clerks, and are seldom so sinful.[1]

These were the Dreamer's doubts. They may represent the poet's
own spiritual dilemma at some period of his life. The temptation to
read them as autobiography is strengthened by the knowledge that
the doubts caused him difficulties in writing his poem. The A-text comes
to an abrupt close here. There is a hasty conclusion, but in it the
Dreamer's questions are not answered.[2] One might speculate that the

5. *The Pardon,* p. 27.
6. x.414–41. Imaginatif solves this difficulty at xii.192–213. See below, p. 64.
7. x.378–89. Imaginatif replies to this point at xii.268–93. See below, p. 65.
8. x.387–9.
9. x.390–413.
1. x.442–74. Imaginatif answers this at xii.72–191. See below, p. 64. Burdach believes
this debate with Scripture and Clergy and particularly the statement that poor plowmen are sooner saved than the learned, parallels the controversy between Piers Plowman and the priest which ends the *Visio: Ackermann,* pp. 306–7. But the subsequent
castigation of the Dreamer for his attitude toward Clergy, and Imaginatif's reply to
this attack on the value of learning for salvation, indicate that the Dreamer's position
here cannot be equated with Piers' position at the end of the *Visio.* Piers' sentiments
are never refuted, but the Dreamer's are. The poet says that the unlettered plowman
will be saved, but considering *Dowel* as a whole I hardly think he says that man's God-
given inwit is a stumbling block and that learning should be abandoned.
2. A.xii, *passim.* Cf. Chambers, *Mind,* pp. 130–1.

poet stopped because the Dreamer's doubts were his own, and he had
not yet resolved them. The mingled distrust and respect for learning
which appears so often in the poem are certainly a reflection of the
poet's attitude. The autobiographical view here is not, however, inevitable. It is just as reasonable to assume that the difficulties were
literary rather than personal. The poet may have found that the intellectual problems he raised were easier to pose than to answer. Or he
may have been unable at first to work out a satisfactory narrative
method for presenting his solutions. The narrative device he creates
in the B-text, it should be said, is both ingenious and satisfying. It is
the dream within a dream. As for the intellectual problems the Dreamer
raised, they are answered in part by a condemnation of the Dreamer's
presumptuousness and in part by an honest intellectual solution of his
difficulties. The condemnation of the Dreamer begins with Scripture's
scornful dismissal, but the real rebuke will be delivered much later by
Imaginatif. In the adventures which befall the Dreamer in the inner
dream there also is an implied rebuke. Imaginatif will solve most of
his difficulties, although the inner dream will solve a few. The real
function of the inner dream, however, is to prepare the Dreamer for
the answers of Imaginatif.

Scorned by Scripture, the Dreamer falls into a dream within his
dream. This dream has four parts: scenes with Fortune and the friars,
Scripture, Trajan, and Kynde and Reason. The Dreamer goes with
Fortune [3] (riches) to the land of longing, where he is promised his
worldly desires. They are joined by Concupiscencia-carnis and Coueytise-
of-eyes, and by Pryde-of-parfyte-lyuynge, who sneers at learning. Elde
(Old Age) warns that these new friends will imperil his soul, but
Recklessness urges him to follow them, and the Dreamer is led away
by Childishness. Elde and Holiness mourn this abandonment of intelligence for the fancies of desire, but for forty-five years the Dreamer
takes no thought of Dowel or Dobet and relies on pardons and prayers
of friars. As he grows old, however, Fortune deserts him, Poverty pur-
sues him, and he quarrels with the friars. They are interested only in
men's money, not their salvation. The scene ends as Lewte (Loyalty?
Justice?) [4] rules that the Dreamer may lawfully tell men the truth about
friars.

The purpose of this scene is to illustrate the delusions of the life
without learning or morality. What must the pillars of such a life be,
the poet asks. The answer is, Fortune and the friars, neither of whom
can be trusted. By experiencing the worthlessness of that kind of life

3. XI.1–102.
4. Donaldson defines "lewte" as " 'exact justice; strict adherence to the letter of the
law.' " In this scene, Lewte "as umpire informs the Dreamer what he may legitimately
tell concerning the abuses practiced by the Friars" (pp. 65–6 and nn. 3–4).

the Dreamer is being prepared to appreciate the advantages of learning and morality. The three characters who assist Fortune in seducing the Dreamer are directly relevant to this theme, as the passage in I John from which they are borrowed shows:

> Nolite diligere mundum, neque ea, quae in mundo sunt. Si quis diligit mundum, non est charitas Patris in eo: quoniam omne, quod est in mundo, concupiscentia carnis est, et concupiscentia oculorum, et superbia vitae: quae non est ex Patre, sed ex mundo est. Et mundus transit, et concupiscentia eius. Qui autem facit voluntatem Dei, manet in aeternum.[5]

The Dreamer had determined to abandon learning and doing well ("non est charitas Patris in eo") and instead to love the things of this world. And what is in the world is Concupiscencia-carnis and Coueytise-of-eyes and Pryde-of-parfite-lyuynge. But even as the epistle warned, the world and desire faded away ("Et mundus transit, et concupiscentia eius"), and the Dreamer was left with his soul in jeopardy. To love the world is not enough.[6]

Scripture now appears and delivers a sermon.[7] It reintroduces the issue of predestination so that it may be briskly disposed of. Her text is Matthew xxii: 1–14: Many were called to a feast, but few were invited in. The Dreamer wonders whether he is one of the elect. But he remembers that he was received at the baptismal font as one of God's chosen, for Christ called all men to come, if they would. In Him is remedy for all sin. Then all men, argues the Dreamer, may claim to sit at this feast of salvation, because of the blood by which Christ bought mankind, and through baptism. Even as the run-away serf belongs to his lord and can be punished by him, so the apostate Christian still belongs to God and will be punished by Him for his misdeeds, unless he is contrite and cries for mercy.[8] Scripture agrees, for books tell

---

5. I John ii: 15–17. Line 16, which is quoted in the Latin *Speculum Christiani*, p. 151, is translated in the Middle English version as follows: "Al *that* es in the worlde, or it is fleschly desyre, outher concupiscence [or] couetyse of een [or] syght, or ellys pride of lyfe" (p. 150). St. Thomas Aquinas discusses these three causes of sin in the *Summa Theologica*, I–II, q. 77, v. Father Dunning cites the passage in the *Summa* and says it was commonly accepted in the Middle Ages: *Piers Plowman*, p. 27, n. 2.

6. Mensendieck thought the scene with Fortune and the Friars was autobiographical: *Charakterentwickelung*, p. 42.

7. XI.103–34.

8. What is the relevance of the serf-Christian analogy? The fact that Christ "bought" mankind with His blood suggests to the poet that the Christian's relation to God is that of human property to owner, i.e. serf to lord. Then *all* Christians belong to God, not a chosen few. But the analogy slides into another topic. The Christian who tries to deny his Christianity and goes about like a "reneyed caityf recchelesly" suggests the Dreamer, for he abandoned Dowel at the suggestion of Recklessness. He, like the serf, however, still belongs to his Lord, and his reason will bring him back to God. (Contrition and God's mercy are apparently discussed in the passage for their own sake.)

men that God's mercy is above all His works. The problem of pre-destination has been solved, and solved so simply that it can hardly have deeply troubled the poet's mind.

Scripture's reference to books brings Trajan, the righteous heathen,[9] into the dream. He is full of scorn for books. He was saved from hell, not by learning or prayers, but by his love and loyalty (or justice?). He is an example of the power for salvation of good works—justice and obedience to the law of love. His long speech [1] is an elaboration on the theme of love, which his story exemplifies. The law of love, he preaches, is all-important. Law without love is worthless, and so is all learning. Above all one must love one's enemies and the poor, as Christ taught. Faith, which Trajan praises above logic and law, means obeying the law of love:

> For sum wordes I fynde ywryten · were of faithes techynge,
> That saued synful men · as seynt Iohan bereth wytnesse;
> *Eadem mensura qua mensi fueritis, remecietur vobis.*
> For-thi lerne we the lawe of loue · as owre lorde tauȝte. . . .[2]

In conclusion, he praises patient poverty as the best way of life.

There are two notable facts about the scene with Trajan. First, there is the turn given to the widely known legend. Chambers points out

---

9. Various versions of the Trajan legend are studied by Gaston Paris, *La Légende de Trajan,* Bibliothèque de l'École pratique des Hautes Études, *35,* Paris, 1878. Refer-ences to the legend are also collected by Sir Israel Gollancz, preface to *St. Erkenwald,* Select Early English Poems, *4* (London, 1922), n. 1, xxxviii–xxxix, xxxviii–l; and by Henry L. Savage, introduction to *St. Erkenwald,* Yale Studies in English, *72* (New Haven, 1926), xvii, nn. 9–10; lxix, n. 48.

1. XI.135–311. There is some question as to who the speaker is for lines 148–310 of this speech. Skeat assigns it to Loyalty (i.e. Lewte). But Lewte is nowhere indicated in the text as the speaker. Line 148 reads, "'Lo, ȝe lordes, what leute did by an em-peroure of Rome. . . .'" This is apparently the basis for Skeat's ascription of the speech to Lewte. In lines 148, 150 f., and 153, Trajan is referred to in the third person rather than in the first person, as we should expect if Trajan were still speaking. This is apparently the reason for assuming that Trajan is not the speaker. This assumption, however, leads to another difficulty. Line 165 reads, "'Lawe with-outen loue,' quod *Troianus,* 'leye there a bene. . . .'" Skeat treats this as a quotation within Lewte's speech and ends Trajan's speech at 167, though there is no inherent logic in stopping it here, for the break comes in the middle of a sentence. It seems more reasonable to assign the whole passage to Trajan, since he is the only speaker indicated in the text. At the close of the speech the Dreamer says, "Ac moche more in metynge thus with me gan one dispute" (XI.311). The "one" here echoes the "one" which opened the Trajan passage: "'ȝee! baw for bokes!' quod one was broken oute of helle. . . ." (XI.135). Lines 148–53 may also be part of Trajan's speech, for a character may refer to himself in the third person. If these lines are not by Trajan, the Dreamer himself would be a more likely candidate for speaker than Skeat's "Loyalty." Chambers assigns the whole speech to the Dreamer (*Mind,* p. 136), as does Donaldson (*Piers Plowman,* p. 173). The speech, however, expresses ideas and doctrines which the Dreamer, at this moment of his education, has not mastered. The purpose of the speech, I believe, is to *teach* the Dreamer these doctrines.

2. XI.220–2.

that later Imaginatif says Trajan never took Christendom, though this is "directly contrary to the later versions of the story, in which Gregory baptizes him." Moreover, the poem "contradicts all known authorities in making Trajan's salvation depend solely upon his own virtues." [3] The treatment also contrasts with that in *St. Erkenwald*, a poem of about the same date, which stresses the celebration of the mass and baptism as necessary for the salvation of a righteous heathen.[4] The poet clearly altered the Trajan story to illustrate the importance for salvation of good works. The speech prepares the way for Imaginatif's assertion that the good heathen might be saved, an assertion which removes a major cause for the Dreamer's skepticism about morality. The second notable fact is the theme of the long discourse. It is a rambling speech, but it rambles along a central highway. Consider the apology at the end:

> This lokynge on lewed prestes · hath don me lepe fram pouerte,
> The whiche I preyse there pacyence is · more parfyt than ricchesse.[5]

Its theme is patient poverty. What begins as a discourse on the law of love ends as a sermon preaching patient poverty, for in the poet's mind these two doctrines are practically identical. Patient poverty is the condition in which, he believes, one may most completely fulfill the law of love.

In the final scene of the inner dream,[6] Kynde shows the Dreamer "the wondres of this worlde." The Dreamer marvels at the knowledge birds and beasts display and is impressed by the way in which Reason rules all creatures except man. But when he asks Reason why he does not guide man likewise so that he will do no wrong, the Dreamer is sternly rebuked. It is no concern of his what Reason allows or disallows. What he needs to learn is the virtue of sufferance. Who is more long-suffering than God, Who might amend all if He wished? He made man weak in nature: *Nemo sine crimine vivit*. The earlier *Nemo bonus* is echoed here, but with a difference.[7]

The main purpose of this scene is to shame the Dreamer and create in him the patience he must possess if he is to continue his spiritual education and progress toward Dowel. The passage immediately following the inner dream states this explicitly. The Dreamer, awakening, reproaches himself, for now he knows that Dowel is to see much

3. Chambers, in *Essays and Studies by Members of the English Association, 9,* 66.

4. Savage, introduction to *St. Erkenwald,* n. 48, pp. lxix–lxx. See also Gollancz, preface to *St. Erkenwald,* pp. liv–lv. *St. Erkenwald* was written ca. 1386; see Savage, pp. lxxv–lxxix, and Gollancz, pp. lvi–lviii.

5. XI.309–10.

6. XI.312–94.

7. In the *Nemo bonus* passage man's imperfection had thrown the Dreamer into a Slough of Despond. Here man's imperfection is shown to be God's work and hence not something for man to pass judgment on or to despair over.

and suffer more (i.e. be patient). Imaginatif appears and tells him that because of his pride and presumption Reason and Clergy both refused to teach him further. He suggests shame as a way of destroying these weaknesses.[8] In the scene with Kynde which concluded the inner dream, the Dreamer's restless desire to know all things and his impatience with the imperfections of humankind, the same traits which led to his original difficulties with Scripture, had brought him to the very peak of presumptuousness: he had questioned the ways of God. When he realized this, he himself was ashamed of his folly. Reason and Imaginatif[9] rebuked him and shamed him, and from them he finally learned what he had to know before he could continue his quest to know the good: there are some aspects of creation which the intelligence must not question, and if God can suffer man to be imperfect, man should be able to suffer it also.

The dream within a dream, for all its variety of incident, centers on one problem, the impasse that arose between the Dreamer and Scripture and Clergy. It arose because of the Dreamer's skepticism about learning and morality. With Fortune and the friars the Dreamer tried the life without learning or morality and found its promises illusory. The experience made the moral life look attractive once more. The scene with Scripture eliminated the doctrine of predestination. It had been an obstacle to belief in the value of intelligence and morality. The scene with Trajan, though it attacked learning, re-emphasized the value of morality, the law of love, and patient poverty. At the same time it suggested that, like Trajan, the righteous heathen might be saved. Finally, the scene with Kynde and Reason shamed the Dreamer into a

---

8. XI.395–431.

9. The usual explanation of Imaginatif as "memory" is unsatisfactory. It was first suggested by Mensendieck, *JEGP, 9,* 405–6, 417; and *ZVgL, 18,* 25, 27. Jones, *JEGP, 13,* 583–8, drew upon the mystical psychology of the Victorines and described Imaginatif as the handmaid of Reason, "gifted with a vision of joy and sorrow to come." The views of Jones and Mensendieck were combined by Chambers: "Long Will," pp. 60–1, and *Mind,* p. 139. For an account of the faculty of imagination in both medieval descriptive psychology and the psychology of the mystics, see Murray Wright Bundy, *The Theory of Imagination in Classical and Mediaeval Thought,* University of Illinois Studies in Language and Literature, *12* (1927), 177–210. Isidore's definition of the soul did not include the faculty of imagination, and so the passage on the soul at xv.23 ff. is of no assistance here. I should like to suggest that by Imaginatif the poet meant the *communis sensus,* "the vertue imaginatiua," which organizes and combines the images perceived by the outer senses, "remembers" these sense impressions, and passes them on to the reason for judgment. The *communis sensus* stands in a direct and superior relationship to the senses, and so might appropriately be chosen by the poet to answer the Dreamer's questions about the value of learning from books ("clergy") and from the senses ("kynde wit"). It also functions as one kind of memory—memory of sense impressions. These functions of "the vertue imaginatiua" are described in Bartholomaeus Anglicus, III, vi, x, xi, xvi; v, iii, x. Randolph Quirk, in a recent brief note, "Vis Imaginativa," *JEGP, 53* (1954), 81–3, agrees with Jones' definition of "imaginatif" as meaning, roughly, "creative reflection," but he does not base his agreement on an analysis of the text or the role of Imaginatif in the poem.

more humble, patient, receptive attitude. These scenes prepare the
Dreamer (and the reader) for the quick solution of the Dreamer's
problems by Imaginatif. The inner dream is clearly integrated into the
didactic narrative.

Imaginatif, the first character the Dreamer meets when he returns
to the original dream, is a faculty of the intellectual soul. Perhaps
Imaginatif is memory; perhaps it is "communis sensus," the overlord
of the senses and depository of what they communicate. Or it may be
creative imagination, as Randolph Quirk suggests. Imaginatif's function in the poem is to resolve the doubts about learning and morality
which the Dreamer raised in the scene with Scripture. Since both
learning and moral action depend on man's possession of an intellectual
soul, Imaginatif shows the Dreamer the uses and limitations of the
human intellect. He discusses "kynde wit," that is, natural intelligence
and what can be learned by the exercise of natural intelligence. And
he discusses "clergy," that is, what can be learned from reading books.
He demonstrates their usefulness for salvation, thus silencing the
Dreamer's suspicion that they were of no value whatsoever. At the
same time he is careful to show their limitations, for it was by asking
more from them than they could provide that the Dreamer became in-
tellectually presumptuous and cynical. Apparently the poet felt it was
difficult to maintain the proper attitude toward the powers of the human
intelligence. He values intelligence as a God-given gift; but his comments on the blasphemous clerks in the lord's hall, the scene with the
logic-chopping friars, and the Dreamer's adventures with Clergy, Scripture, and Reason show him to have been very sensitive to intellectual
arrogance.

Imaginatif first establishes the limitations of kynde wit and clergy.[1]
Charity, which is Dowel and wins salvation, is contrasted with kynde
wit (and riches), which often result in misery and damnation. Then
grace is contrasted with kynde wit and clergy (and riches again): grace
enables man to love, but it grows among the poor, not the rich.[2] Clergy

---

1. XII.30–71.

2. The talk about riches is extraneous, for the real issue is the value of clergy and
kynde wit. But the poet cannot keep riches out of the poem. Perhaps there is an implication that clergy and kynde wit, if valued for their own sake, are as destructive of the
soul's health as riches are. Theologians, moralists, and even encyclopedists, while prais-
ing reason, loved also to stress its limitations as compared to God's limitless knowledge;
its inability to know the essential truths, which were matters of faith; and the danger
of overcuriosity. Cf. *Summa Theologica*, I, q. 94, iii, and II–II, q. 8, iii, to give just two
references from Aquinas. Cf. also the warning against overcuriosity in *Speculum Christiani*, p. 12, and against believing too much in natural reason in matters of faith, p. 180.
Cf. also the distinction made between "middle goods," such as clear wit, good understanding, great memory, etc., which are useful but do not win salvation, and "true
goods," such as grace, charity, and virtue: *Vices and Virtues*, pp. 77–8. The same book
also warns against the proud or presumptuous man who thinks he knows more than
others (p. 17), and says "þe wit of þe world is folye, for he þat weneþ clerly to see is

and kynde wit can be explained; they are no mystery. But grace is, and neither kynde wit nor clergy can explain it.

Now Imaginatif can proceed to show their real usefulness.[3] They help man to amend, and they are his guides. Clergy he praises especially. Kynde wit by itself cannot save a man,[4] but books, which are inspired by God and the Holy Ghost, can. Though some ignorant men are more easily saved than kynde-witted or learned men, usually it is easier for the man with learning to secure salvation.

The Dreamer had argued with Scripture that morality was value-less for salvation because evil persons like Dismas the thief were saved. Imaginatif now meets this issue.[5] Dismas was saved because he asked God for grace, which is granted freely to all who wish to amend. More important, Imaginatif says those of evil life who are saved sit not high in heaven. There are degrees of reward in heaven, and those of worthier life receive greater rewards.[6] Morality *is* of value in the scheme of salvation. But the topic returns to the theme of the limitations of kynde wit and clergy. They cannot tell man why Dismas was saved and not the other thief, why Reason rules beasts but not always men, why nature is so various and complex. Only Kynde, God the Creator, knows the answers. It is enough for man to know that these things are His work.[7] Yet a moral purpose is perceptible. The complex world of nature gives man lessons for salvation,[8] which he perceives by his kynde wit: he learns from nature the law of love, patient poverty.

Imaginatif also establishes the value of morality and learning by his

---

starke blynd" (p. 69), and speaks of the vanity of learning ("Witt of clergie"), e.g. "þe verrey witt þat þe Holy Gost techeþ to Godes frendes is to knowe and nouȝt mys-take al þing what it is worþ" (pp. 80-1). The *Mirrour of the World* of Gautier of (or Gossouin) Metz, ed. Oliver H. Prior, EETS, e.s. *110* (London, 1913), while full of the praises of reason, insists again and again on its limitations: pp. 47, 97, 104 f.

3. XII.72-191.

4. Cf. *Vices and Virtues*, pp. 69-70: Wise philosophers hated this world and desired immortality so much "þat soutilede þei and studiede of here owne wittes and willes, but al was for nouȝt." Cf. also p. 124.

5. XII.192-267.

6. St. Thomas Aquinas teaches that there are degrees in heaven: *Summa Theologica*, II-II, q. *28*, iii (ad. 2). Carleton F. Brown in "The Author of *The Pearl*, Considered in the Light of his Theological Opinions," *PMLA*, *19* (1904), 127-45, argued that the contemporary *Pearl*-poet preached the equality of heavenly reward. This view was strongly attacked by J. B. Fletcher in "The Allegory of the Pearl," *JEGP*, *20* (1921), 17-18.

7. Cf. *Mirrour of the World*, p. 105: "And therfor he is a fool that meruaylleth of thynges that God maketh; ffor noo creature hath the power to shewe reson wherfore they ben or not; ffor ther is nothyng, how lytil it be, that the glose may be knowen vnto the trouthe, sauf only that whiche pleseth to Our Lord God. Ffor to be wel founded in clergye may men knowe & vnderstande the reson of somme thinges, and also by na-ture suche thinge as by reson can not be comprehended. Thawh a man enquyre neuer so longe of that is wrought in therthe by nature, he shal not mowe come to the knowel-ege wherefore ne how they be made. This may noman certaynly knowe, sauf God only whiche knoweth the reson and vnderstondeth it."

8. Cf. ibid., p. 47, where it is stated that God gave man wit and understanding that he might learn from nature what was evil, avoid it, and lead the good life.

solution of the problem of the righteous heathen.[9] If Aristotle and other learned, righteous clerks were not saved, the Dreamer had said, what good was learning and morality? No one knows whether they are saved, Imaginatif confesses, but since God is good and God gave them the kynde wit by which they taught mankind moral lessons from examples in nature,[1] men should pray that He will grant them salvation. Imaginatif insists on the possibility of their salvation because of their good lives. He quotes from I Peter, "saluabitur vix iustus in die iudicij." The fact that the just are *scarcely* ("vix") saved must mean they are saved. Trajan was never baptized and he is saved. The man who faithfully obeys his (religious) law and never breaks it, who knows no better law (Christianity) but would follow it if he knew it— surely a true God would commend him.[2]

With this daring hope[3] Imaginatif concludes his defense of intelligence and learning and the moral action which they lead to. His last words, before he vanishes and the first vision of *Dowel* ends, are words of praise for wit and wisdom.

The first vision of *Dowel* has focused on one activity of the intel-

9. XII.268–90.

1. Cf. the extended praise of the ancients for their love of learning in *Mirrour of the World*, pp. 16–29, and such statements as the following: "yf clergye had be loste, we had knowen nothing ne who had be God, ne men shold neuer haue knowen what thing had ben best to doo: and so shold alle the world haue ben dampned. Thenne had we ben born in an euyll houre, ffor the men had knowen nomore than do dombe beestis" (p. 28).

2. See Skeat's explication of this passage, *Parallel Texts, 2,* 188.

3. In "Langland and the Salvation of the Heathen," *MedAev, 12* (1943), 45–54, Father Dunning argues that the poet was not unorthodox in suggesting that the righteous heathen could be saved, for the scholastics taught that God might by divine inspiration teach the righteous heathen those principles of faith necessary for salvation. As for baptism, the other requisite for salvation, there was baptism by the Holy Ghost as well as by water and by blood. But while referring vaguely to baptism by the Holy Ghost, the poet does not comply with the rest of the doctrine which Father Dunning outlines, for he has the righteous heathen saved, if he is saved, not by knowing the principles of faith through divine inspiration, but by adhering obediently to the best faith he knows. And Chambers has justly remarked that the doctrine that the righteous heathen might be saved could not have been common knowledge in the Middle Ages, or Langland and Dante would not have struggled so with the problem: *Mind,* pp. 146–7. See also his "Dante, Long Will, and the Righteous Heathen," *passim.* Cf. *Vices and Virtues,* pp. 69–70, 77–8, 124, and for additional contemporary material, Mary Edith Thomas, *Medieval Skepticism and Chaucer* (New York, 1950), pp. 64–71. A prominent Benedictine monk contemporary with *Piers Plowman,* Uthred of Boldon, was also concerned with the problem. He developed the doctrine of the clara visio, the opinion that all human beings, Christians, Jews, Saracens, pagans, adults, children, or still-born infants, at the moment immediately preceding death had a "clear vision" of God, by the light of that vision chose or rejected God, and in so doing determined their lot for eternity. The doctrine involved Boldon in a controversy at Oxford with the friars. It was condemned November 9, 1368, by Simon Langham, Archbishop of Canterbury. See M. D. Knowles, "The Censured Opinions of Uthred of Boldon," *Proceedings of the British Academy, 37* (1951), 305–42. See also Mildred Elizabeth Marcett, *Uthred de Boldon, Friar William Jordan, and "Piers Plowman"* (New York, 1938), esp. pp. 30, 32, 44–6. But Knowles' essay is theologically more expert, and he gives a corrected text of the condemned propositions, together with the relevant censure from Wilkins' *Concilia.*

lectual soul, the activity of knowing, what the poet calls wit (Kynde Wit) and learning (Clergy). It has shown the role which wit and learning play in the scheme of salvation. It has revealed that by his intellectual soul man arrives at a knowledge of the basic moral law, the law of love and the doctrine of patient poverty. If man does not obey this law, he cannot be saved. And he cannot obey it, of course, unless he knows it. But the primary purpose is not to teach this law in detail. That will be done in the next vision. The narrative here has been organized to show that man's wit and learning help him to save his soul. The poet does this by taking as his plot the search for information about Dowel. This leads naturally to speeches about Dowel. In some of these, the Dreamer is told that his wit and learning enable him to do well. More important, the answers about Dowel come from characters who are either faculties of the intellectual soul—Thought, Wit, Imaginatif (and Reason)—or aspects of learning—Dame Study, Scripture, and Clergy. The names of the characters reveal that wit and learning inform man of the rules of moral action.

The search for Dowel is given a brilliant turn when the Dreamer doubts the value of wit and learning. This development enables the poet to examine their role in the scheme of salvation in a new and exciting form. It enables him to answer a number of basic questions about wit and learning and to argue their importance in the dramatic scenes of the inner dream and the speeches of Reason and Imaginatif. At the same time he is able to raise the issue of intellectual presumptuousness. To the Dreamer's attack on wit and learning because they leave man still immoral, Imaginatif and Reason reply that man's imperfection is suffered by God; wit and learning were not intended to make man perfect. To his complaint that they do not enable man to know the reason for all things, Imaginatif and Reason reply that this limitation is also part of God's plan and therefore good. Their purpose is not to search out the secrets of nature, but to enable man to know what is good for the soul. If they teach man what is necessary for his salvation, what higher knowledge can there be? To the Dreamer's argument that intellect and learning are useless, for their fruit, morality, does not save man's soul—a conclusion suggested by the doctrine of predestination, the fate of the righteous heathen, and the salvation of the wicked—a reply is given in the scene with Fortune and the friars, in the rejection of predestination, and in Imaginatif's statement that there are degrees of bliss in heaven. The climactic argument, however, is his assertion that the righteous heathen is saved. If the heathen may be saved for his righteousness, surely moral effort must avail. And since morality is impossible without the intellectual soul's activity of knowing, without wit and learning, these do help toward salvation.

The first vision concentrated on showing how man *knows* the good.

The second vision reveals how man *does* the good. The fourteenth
century *Book of Vices and Virtues* says "þese tweie þinges sauen a man :
whan he leueþ wel and a-riȝt, and doþ þer-after as he scholde." [4] Having shown how God has enabled man to fulfill the first of these require-
ments, the poet now shows how God has enabled him to fulfill the
second. The protagonists of the second vision, Conscience and Patience,
relate to man's actions rather than to his knowledge. The doctrines
the vision teaches are love, *ne solliciti sitis,* patient poverty, and penance.
In the first vision of *Dowel* patient poverty was identified with the law
of love. Here penance and patient poverty and *ne solliciti sitis* are intertwined with one another and with the law of love. Patient poverty, the
way of life which best enables a man to obey the law of love, is the
probable consequence of obeying the injunction *ne solliciti sitis.* Certainly the doctrine of *ne solliciti sitis* strengthens patience in poverty.
Patient poverty is at the same time a kind of penance on this earth.
And penance is ever necessary for man if he would be saved, for he is
sinful by nature and his soul constantly requires cleansing.

This view of man's sinfulness is not, of course, peculiar to the poem.
It was the view of most medieval moralists. The fourteenth-century
author of *The Book of Vices and Virtues* said : "aȝens oureself we ben
so pore and so feble þat we ne myȝt neuere an houre of a day suffre
þe assaut of þe deuel wiþ-out help of oure lord, & whan he faileþ vs
we fallen yn a-swiþe, & whan he helpeþ vs we wiþstondeþ and fiȝtteþ &
ouercomen." [5] The poet, of course, is asserting in *Dowel* that man can
do well, but his sense of man's weakness is very strong. So in the
present vision, where he is showing how man is able to do what is
good, he stresses penance. Though this may seem a negative approach,
his age considered penance a positive moral action : "seynt Gregori seiþ,
'Verrey doynge is not to speke faire wordes wiþ þe mouþ, but to make
gret compleynt for synne and þerwiþ sore syȝynges of herte.' " [6]

The waking interlude serves as a bridge between the first and second
visions.[7] It summarizes the adventure in the inner dream with Fortune
and the friars and some of the teachings of Imaginatif. If there is any
link between the interlude and doctrinal elements in the second vision,
it is very obscure.[8] The Dreamer walking abroad like a mendicant may
be an image foreshadowing the doctrines of *ne solliciti sitis* and patient
poverty. The recapitulation of the experiences with Fortune and the
friars and of Imaginatif's lessons seems to be memory at work, perhaps
the aftereffect of Imaginatif in his function as memory warning the

4. P. 98.
5. P. 115.
6. Ibid., pp. 97-8.
7. XIII.1–20.
8. Donaldson, pp. 151–3, discusses the possibility that XIII.1–3 and similar passages
(XV.3–10, XVIII.1–3, and Pr. 123) have an autobiographical significance.

Dreamer against evil ways and making him desire to do good. The vision itself will be concerned with the problem of putting moral doctrine into practice. Also, true contrition and confession will be taught in the vision, and memory is essential in these processes. (Memory makes "mone to god," the poet says elsewhere.) [9] The stressing of God's love for His creatures may point toward the complete reliance on God's love which Conscience and Patience advise—the doctrines of *ne solliciti sitis* and patient poverty.

Falling asleep, the Dreamer meets Conscience, one of the heroes of the poem. In another passage the poet quotes Isidore of Seville on conscience, *"dum negat vel consentit, Consciencia est;"* and translates this as "And whan I chalange or chalange nouʒte, chepe or refuse, Thanne am I Conscience ycalde, goddis clerke and his notarie. . . ." [1] The elaboration on the Latin underlines the importance of Conscience. He is God's notary. He controls man's acts, accepting or rejecting proposed courses of action.[2] Conscience invites the Dreamer to a dinner at which Clergy, Scripture, a learned doctor from the friars, and Patience, a poor pilgrim, are present. The pilgrim's role indicates that patience is associated with the poverty and humility of the true pilgrim, and the courteous reception of Patience by Conscience means that man's conscience accepts patience as a good way of life. The Dreamer has acquired this virtue, for he sits with Patience at the feast.

The dinner scene [3] focuses in its first half on the Doctor.[4] He is a masterly creation, an arch-hypocrite whose devotion to things of the flesh is matched only by the enormous brashness with which he utters spiritual truths. Through him the poet makes his first point about *doing* good—that knowing what is good is not enough. Knowledge must be transformed into action. The theme of the preceding vision—knowing the good—is thus merged with the theme of this vision—doing the good.

A number of contrasts are set up in the scene to make the point. All of them involve the Doctor, and they give the scene a richly ironic tone. The first is one of position. The Doctor sits at the high table; the Dreamer and Patience sit humbly at a side table. The Doctor's pride is thus set off against patient humility, which he should practice.[5] There is a contrast also in the dinner fare of the two groups of

9. xv.26.

1. xv.31-2. The Latin is given after xv.39.

2. Cf. also the important role which Conscience plays in *Dobest*. See below, Chapter 6.

3. xiii.21-214.

4. Miss Marcett, pp. 57-64, has argued that the Doctor is a caricature of a contemporary, friar William Jordan. Aubrey Gwynn, "The Date of the B-Text of *Piers Plowman*," *RES, 19* (1943), 19-24, also discusses this possibility.

5. The use of the dinner scene and of differences in seating to illustrate patient humility in contrast to pride was probably suggested by Luke xiv: 8-11, in which Christ advises the guests at a feast to sit not in the highest room, but in the lowest. The

guests. The Doctor's rich food reveals that he will not live by the great religious teachings but instead accepts ill-gotten gains, for which he will suffer after death. The food of Patience and the Dreamer is humility, contrition, confession—in short, penance. The life which continues in sin, does no penance, and leads to punishment after death is being contrasted with the life of penance by which man is cleansed of his sins before death. But these contrasts are really preparatory to the principal contrast in the scene, that between knowing about the good life and leading the good life. It is exposed in the clash between what the Doctor does about penance and what he says about it. Only four days ago he preached on St. Paul's penance, but he doesn't practice penance himself. The clash is even sharper in the doctor's definitions of Dowel. It is to do no evil to your fellow Christian, he says between sips—but he has done evil himself by his gluttony. More impertinent is his statement that Dowel does what clerks teach, Dobet teaches others, and Dobest does as he himself teaches.[6]

Because the Doctor is a lost soul, it does not follow that he gives bad advice. The advice is, in fact, very good. The Doctor is certainly modeled on the scribes and Pharisees in Matthew xxiii : 2–6, who, like the Doctor, love the chief place at feasts : "Amant autem primos recubitus in coenis." Like the Doctor, they know what is good, and so should be obeyed, but like him, they do not practice what they preach : "Omnia ergo quaecumque dixerint vobis, seruate, et facite : secundum opera vero eorum nolite facere : dicunt enim, et non faciunt." Therefore, although the Doctor's teaching is sound, its main purpose is to warn the reader of the necessity of doing good as well as knowing it. The cream of the jest is that men are told to practice what they preach by the man who above all others fails to do just that.

In unmasking the Doctor, Conscience has started a kind of question bee about Dowel,[7] which may mean that man's conscience tries to know what is good in order to perform it. The answer Clergy gives to Conscience is strikingly hesitant. Piers Plowman, he says, has questioned all sciences, save love alone, and has taken as his only text, *dilige deum,* and *domine, quis habitabit, &c.*[8] Piers says that Dowel and Dobet are

position of the Doctor and the traits he displays were probably suggested by Matthew xxiii : 2–6, in which Christ speaks of the hypocrisy of the Pharisees and of their love for the chief place at feasts. The two passages are linked, not only by the topic of seating positions at feasts, but also by Luke xiv : 11 and Matthew xxiii : 12, which express identical sentiments about pride and humility in almost identical language.

6. XIII.64–117. The Doctor's definitions of Dowel, Dobet, and Dobest do not hint at the Three Lives. Teaching others (Dobet) was enjoined on all Christians : cf. *Speculum Christiani*, pp. 3–7, 44, 98, 124–6.

7. XIII.118–32.

8. This is a favorite quotation of the poet's, from a favorite psalm, Psalm xiv (Vulgate). It supplies the basic doctrine of the *Visio:* it is used at II.38, III.233 ff., and VII.41, 51. The psalm asserts that the man of good life will be saved. Included in the description of the righteous man is the virtue of love. II.34–8 seems to indicate that the poet associated the psalm with the doctrine of charity.

two infinites which, with a faith, find Dobest, which shall save man's soul. This last is apparently meant to be unintelligible, for Conscience says he does not understand it. Any doctrine which comes from Piers has authority, however; of that we can be certain.

Conscience now queries Patience, saying he knows what no clerk knows, for "Pacientes vincunt." One important lesson in this vision is the virtue of patience. It was sadly lacking in the Dreamer in the first vision of *Dowel*. He has been shown slowly acquiring it in the dinner scene, writhing under the Doctor's hypocrisies but keeping silent at Patience's command. The importance of patience appears in the speech here in response to Conscience (the speech is given by Piers Plowman himself in the C-text).[9] Patience expounds clearly and firmly what Clergy advanced tentatively and obscurely, Piers' doctrine, the law of love.[1] Dowel, Dobet, and Dobest, he says, are *Disce, Doce, Dilige inimicos*.[2] All three commands are good, but Patience elaborates only on the command to love. He stresses, as has not been done before, the necessity of loving one's enemy. This, of course, is the most difficult command to obey in the law of love, and it is appropriate that Patience should expound it. Patience and love become one and the same thing in his speech. There is in the speech some of the deliberate mystification that the poet at times could not resist.[3] Nevertheless, Patience teaches effectively the importance of love, concluding with the assertion that poverty or enemies will not grieve a man if he loves, for *"Caritas nichil timet."* There is a preparation here for *ne solliciti sitis* and patient poverty.

The worldly Doctor cannot appreciate this reliance on love. "Nothing can make peace between a pope and his enemies or between two Christian kings,"[4] he says, a reminder that others, too, know the law and do not obey it. With this the dinner party begins to break up. The attitude toward learning which the farewell scene[5] reflects is most interesting. It is the same mixed attitude apparent in the scene with the friars at the beginning of *Dowel* and in the crisis over wit and learning. Imaginatif had praised learning, and in the dinner scene the Dreamer has been most respectful of Clergy. But the figure of the learned Doctor has revealed that to know is not necessarily to do, and

9. C.xvi.138–48.

1. xiii.133–71.

2. This is the famous definition which some critics have accepted as *the* explanation of the three terms. All three commands would apply to every Christian.

3. xiii.152–6, omitted in the C-text.

4. xiii.172–6. Skeat did not think the remark about the pope was a reference to the Great Schism: *Parallel Texts, 2,* 198. J. A. W. Bennett, on the other hand, argues that it is, and that the reference to war between two Christian kings refers to the war between the French and the English, which had broken out again in 1377: "The Date of the B-Text of *Piers Plowman,*" *MedAev, 12* (1943), 60–1.

5. xiii.176–214.

Clergy's hesitant answer about Dowel contrasts with the forthright reply of Patience. The farewell scene implies yet more clearly that learning by itself is limited in value. For Conscience allies himself with Patience rather than with Clergy and chooses penance and love rather than learning alone. This means that there comes a time when man must go beyond learning and try to put his knowledge into practice. With conscience as his guide, man must seek to master the virtue of patience. With patience, he can sincerely love God and mourn for his sins. And if mankind were patiently to apply its knowledge in accordance with the dictates of conscience, the world would become a wondrous place [6]—the apocalyptic vision again! Learning is very important, for the Christian needs it to be confirmed in the true faith. But it is more important for man to put his learning to use and perfect his conscience with patience.

The scene with the Doctor has illustrated one difficulty in the process of doing good. The scene with Haukyn which follows illustrates another. Conscience and Patience set forth as pilgrims. Talking of Dowel, they meet Haukyn, Activa Vita, the breadwinner of the world who feeds mankind. He is a simple, hard-working, literal-minded fellow who thinks he knows how to reform mankind: Just deny it enough of the bread he sweats so hard to make! Haukyn in his way is as great a creation as the Doctor. The poet, in describing Haukyn's sins, uses the personification form with a daring freedom. Haukyn is not only a waferer, but a beggar, a money-lender, a merchant, and a plowman.[7] Nevertheless he remains a convincing, realistic character, largely because he is so consistently vigorous and earthbound. Haukyn's association with bread is reminiscent of Gregory's description of the Active Life as "panem esurienti tribuere." [8] It suggests a contrast with the spiritual bread prayed for in the Pater Noster, perhaps even with the wafer of the mass. The contrast points up Haukyn's worldliness. Haukyn also calls to mind Christ's warning that man cannot live by bread alone, for Haukyn has been so concerned with supplying bread for the body that he has neglected his soul. That is the poet's main purpose in creating Haukyn: to show how living in the world, breadwinning, the Active Life, inevitably involves man in sin. Haukyn's coat of Christendom is spotted and soiled with the seven deadly sins.[9]

For Haukyn's sinfulness there are three remedies, to be taken together: penance, the doctrine of *ne solliciti sitis* (already stated by Piers in the pardon scene), and patient poverty. The first of these is recom-

6. XIII.215-71.
7. XIII.303, 357-61, 362, 371-3.
8. For the complete quotation from Gregory see above, p. 10.
9. XIII.272-458. Haukyn's soiled coat may have been suggested by the image in Jude 23: "eam, quae carnalis est, maculatam tunicam."

mended by Conscience, who tells Haukyn that Dowel, Dobet, and Dobest are contrition, confession, and satisfaction.[1] Then Patience merges Conscience's doctrine of contrition with the doctrine of *ne solliciti sitis.* The combining agent is firm belief, for both are the consequence of faith. *Ne solliciti sitis* is the command which man is told to follow when caring for his bodily needs. To obey it is to resign himself to the will of God, as man promises to do in the Pater Noster: *fiat voluntas tua.* This is an act of faith. And faith leads to contrition also. Faith, therefore, will assist man in avoiding sin in this world, for the faithful man, obeying the command *ne solliciti sitis,* will not be so often led into sin by concern for bodily needs. Man's faith will also cleanse him when he does sin, for, moved by his conscience, the faithful man will be contrite.[2]

In a second speech Patience explains patient poverty to Haukyn.[3] Charity, he tells him, dwells with patient poverty. Patient poverty has three spiritual advantages over riches: the poor man has a claim to happiness in the next world because he has had none in this;[4] the poor have prior claim to God's comfort for mankind, the forgiveness of sins;[5] finally, riches are an invitation to sin, but poverty is a protection against it.[6] Then he gives Haukyn a description of patient poverty taken from Vincent de Beauvais' *Speculum Historiale.*[7] The first and last points are important. Poverty is *"odibile bonum"* because, even as contrition is both a sorrow and solace to the soul, so poverty is both penance and joy, for it brings spiritual health to the body. Poverty and penance are equated.[8] Poverty is also *"absque solicitudine*

---

1. XIII.459–XIV.27. The line from Luke xiv: 20, which Haukyn quotes at XIV.3, is appropriate but should not be misinterpreted. In the passage in Luke, Christ warns that those who will not renounce worldly ties and cares to follow Him will not be saved— the message that Patience is about to preach. This is not, however, a counsel to take up the Contemplative Life, according to the commentaries on the passage in the *Catena Aurea,* v, 509–20. Bede's commentary on Luke xiv: 33 illuminates the point of the passage: "But there is a difference between renouncing all things and leaving all things. For it is the way of few perfect men to leave all things, that is, to cast behind them the cares of the world, but it is the part of all the faithful to renounce all things, that is, so to hold the things of the world as by them not to be held in the world" (p. 520).

2. XIV.28–96.
3. XIV.97–319.
4. XIV.103–80.
5. XIV.181–200.
6. XIV.201–72.
7. XIV.275–319.
8. Skeat's gloss on this passage is misleading: " 'Poverty is . . . health to the body.' " *The Vision of William Concerning Piers the Plowman . . . ,* Text B, ed. W. W. Skeat, EETS, o.s. *38* (London, 1869), XIV.283–4. The point really is, I believe, that poverty is *spiritual* health to the body. There is a parallelism between contrition and poverty. Contrition is a condition of the soul, and poverty is a condition of the body. Contrition is related to penance, and so is poverty: it is a form of physical penance. Contrition is good for the soul's spiritual health. Poverty is good for the body's spiritual health, because it makes the body a help toward salvation rather than a hindrance, as it is when man is too solicitous about his bodily needs. Haukyn's example has shown this.

felicitas." Here is the doctrine of *ne solliciti sitis* again: patience is
bread for poverty, sobriety is his drink. Poverty is "a blissed lyf with-
outen bysynesse. . . ."[9] When he realizes how often he has sinned
because he has not followed the life of patient poverty, Haukyn regrets
his possessions and his sinful life. As the contrite Haukyn weeps, the
Dreamer wakens. *Dowel* is at an end.[1]

Understanding the scene with Haukyn depends in large part on
understanding that many of the doctrines taught here were commonplace in medieval religious and moral teaching. What is more, they
were addressed to all men. They had their roots in the Bible, and all
were flourishing in the poet's time. Penance was a duty of all men,
to which, indeed, their very nature called them, for conscience in man
leads to penance. A man may see his sins, says a fourteenth-century
moralist, "in þe booke of his herte" if "he wole wel studie and write
in his herte and in his conscience."[2] And seeing his sins, man is moved
to sorrow and penance. Contrition, confession, and satisfaction were,
of course, the orthodox divisions of penance. The virtue of patience was
likewise recommended by the Bible and by moralists. It is recommended by the example of Christ and of God (Reason reminded the
Dreamer of God's patience in the inner dream), by the beatitudes and
many other texts, and by a host of commentators and moralists.[3] It
was, like penance, a commonplace doctrine. Patience was frequently
associated with poverty, as it is in *Piers Plowman.* Poverty is, of
course, often discussed separately as a virtue. It, too, was recommended
by the example of Christ Himself, by a beatitude,[4] by biblical texts,[5]
and by moralists.[6] The virtue of poverty is also praised by implication
in the many attacks on riches in the Bible, the Fathers, and the moral-

9. xiv.316. Cf. also 300–5, " '*absque solicitudine semita.*' "
1. xiv.320–32.
2. *Vices and Virtues,* p. 40. The sins of covetousness are referred to specifically, but
the statement holds for all sins.
3. Petrus Cantor has a chapter, "De patientia," *Verbum Abbreviatum,* PL, *205,* cols.
298–305, in which are gathered biblical texts in praise of patience together with observations by Cantor himself. He cites the patience of God and the patience of Christ. He
begins with the beatitude commending patience, and his own words indicate the importance of patience in medieval ethics: " 'Beati qui persecutionem patiuntur propter
justitiam, quoniam merces eorum copiosa est in coelo (*Matth.* v).' Septem tantum
sunt beatitudines perfectae consummantes scalem Jacob (*Gen.* xxviii) . . . ; verum
praeter has restat patientia, quae octava redit ad caput circumeundo, purificando, pro-
bando et manifestando omnes virtutes. Sicut enim aurum in fornace, ita et hac omnis
virtus probatur" (col. 298). For some other moralists on patience see *Speculum
Christiani,* pp. 196, 198, 200; *Vices and Virtues,* p. 66; *Mirrour of the Blessed Lyf,* pp.
64–5, 81; and, to indicate the range, Bartholomaeus Anglicus, Bk. I.
4. Luke vi:21; and also Matthew v:3. In the poem these two texts are apparently
combined: cf. xiv.214.
5. See those collected by Petrus Cantor, PL, *205,* cols. 65–70.
6. Cf. *Speculum Christiani,* pp. 66–8; *Mirrour of the Blessed Lyf,* pp. 47 f., 53,
68–9, 70, 110; "The Castel of Love," lines 853–8, in Vol. *1* of *Minor Poems of the
Vernon MS.,* ed. Carl Horstmann, EETS, o.s. *98,* London, 1892. The castle ditch in
the poem is of suffering poverty, by which the Devil is overcome.

ists.[7] Since patience must have an object, and since poverty calls for patience, the two doctrines were often taught as one. The New Testament supplies authority for the doctrine of patient poverty in the example of Christ, in the beatitude "Beati pauperes spiritu," and perhaps most strikingly in the epistle of James, a great part of which moves back and forth between praises of patience on the one hand and praises of poverty and warnings to the rich on the other.[8] The association of patience with poverty in the fourteenth century is well illustrated by the contemporary alliterative poem *Patience,* which may, indeed, have influenced the author of *Piers Plowman* to value patient poverty so highly.[9] In *Patience* the poet recites the eight beatitudes from Matthew and then comments:

> He were happen þat hade one, alle were þe better!
> Bot [s]yn I am put to a poynt þat Pouerte hatte,
> I schal me poruay Pacyence, & play me wyth boþe:
>
> For in þe tyxte, þere þyse two arn in teme layde,
> Hit arn fettled in on forme, þe forme & þe laste,
> & by quest of her quoyntyse enquylen on mede;
> & als, in myn vpynyoun, hit arn of on kynde:
>
> For þer as Pouert hir proferes, ho nyl be put vtter,
> Bot lenge where-so euer hir lyst, lyke oþer greme;
> & þere as Pouert enpresses, þaʒ mon pyne þynk,
> Much, maugre his mun, he mot nede suffer.
>
> Thus Pouerte & Pacyence arn nedes play-feres.[1]

And the poem concludes:

> For-þy when pouerte me enpreceʒ & payneʒ in-noʒe,
> Ful softly wyth suffraunce saʒttel me bihoueʒ,
> For þe penaunce & payne to preue hit in syʒt,—
> Þat pacience is a nobel poynt, þaʒ hit displese ofte.[2]

The doctrine of patient poverty was apparently current at the time.[3] Finally, the doctrine of *ne solliciti sitis* is really a counsel, by implica-

---

7. Cf. *Speculum Christiani,* pp. 126, 222–4; *Vices and Virtues,* pp. 76–7.

8. For praises of patience see James i: 3, 4; v: 7–8, 10–11; for praises of poverty and warnings against riches see i: 9–11; ii: 1–9, esp. 5; and v: 1–6.

9. See Menner's introduction to *Purity,* p. xxix.

1. *Patience,* ed. Sir Israel Gollancz, Select Early English Poems, *1* (London, 1913), lines 34–45.

2. Ibid., lines 528–31.

3. Cf. *Mirrour of the Blessed Lyf,* pp. 130–1. The praises of "glad poverte" in the *Wife of Bath's Tale* (D, 1177–1204), including the same passage from Vincent de Beauvais that appears in *Piers Plowman,* are further striking evidence of the currency of the doctrine and its secular implications.

tion, to patient poverty. The doctrine itself was not unknown. The commentaries on the text [4] and Konrad Burdach's investigation of the history of the doctrine in the Old and New Testament and in Augustine and other medieval writers [5] show that in using this text the poet was preaching what had been preached by many before him and would have a familiar ring for many of his readers.

The particular combination of these doctrines in the poem and the emphasis they receive is the poet's own creation. The stress on patient poverty and on *ne solliciti sitis* is extreme and mystical. Obviously there is a call to reform and to a new way of life here. But the call is to put familiar teachings into practice. The teachings in themselves would not suggest the contemplative life to a fourteenth-century audience, and for all his extremism, the poet would have to commend the contemplative life explicitly if that was his message. If one understands that these counsels to penance and patient poverty were almost commonplaces to men in the fourteenth century, one can understand their significance in the poem. Otherwise, because they are so alien to the spirit of twentieth-century Western culture, they are liable to be misinterpreted as revolutionary calls to abandon the world, manifestoes of asceticism. Even so sensitive a scholar as R. W. Chambers has fallen into this error. Just as he thought Piers' appeal to the birds of the field in the pardon scene was a pledge to become a contemplative, so he explains Patience's speeches here as a summons to that same way of life. And so he writes:

> Hawkyn, Active Life, stands for all, from the lowest to the highest, who are too 'fleshly and boisterous', too much cumbered with the world, to undertake the life of Contemplation, Poverty and Charity. Piers had been qualified, Hawkyn is *not*.
>
> So Hawkyn passes out of the story, sobbing; and Piers, the Active Life which is fitted to become Contemplative, is once more the Protagonist.[6]

Against this view it may be urged, first, that it misreads the conclusion of the vision, for the tears and penitence of Haukyn, and his regret that he ever had property, certainly mean that he has accepted Patience's teaching of patient poverty. Secondly, it may be argued that if the poem were turning here from the Active Life to the Con-

---

4. See above, p. 31.
5. For the references to Burdach see above, p. 32, n. 9.
6. *Mind*, p. 154; and cf. p. 151. See also Donaldson, *Piers Plowman*, pp. 175–6; and Stella Maguire, "The Significance of Haukyn, *Activa Vita*, in *Piers Plowman*," *RES*, 25 (1949), 98. I prefer Burdach's conclusion that the scene with Haukyn teaches that "Piers plowman ist nicht gleichbedeutend mit der vita activa. Er ist mehr. Er ist eine besondere, höhere Bewährung dieser vita activa." *Ackermann*, p. 304. But it is still the active life, not the contemplative, that the poem is concerned with.

templative, there would be some treatment of that way of life to balance
the analysis of the Active Life presented through Haukyn. But there
is no character named or symbolizing the Contemplative Life in the
poem. And I shall try to demonstrate that there is no dramatization
of that way of life in *Dobet*. But the really important error in Chambers' position is that he misunderstands the significance of Patience's
teachings for the fourteenth century. A fourteenth-century reader, to
whom these doctrines would be more or less familiar moral advice,
would require something more than the mere preaching of penance and
patient poverty before he would see that the Contemplative Life was
being urged upon him here. The medieval commentaries on *ne solliciti
sitis* did not interpret it as a call to abandon active labor and become
a contemplative, and the passage quoted from *Patience* reveals no association between patient poverty and the life of contemplation. The
complete absence of any reference in Patience's speeches to contemplatives indicates clearly enough that he is not talking about the Contemplative Life. The doctrines he does preach were, as a matter of fact,
associated, not with the Contemplative Life, but with the Active Life.
Burdach has shown that the doctrines of *ne solliciti sitis* and of poverty
were specifically associated in the medieval period with the idealization
of labor.[7]

The scene with Haukyn is not designed, then, to establish the
superiority of the Contemplative Life. What Haukyn with his spotted
garment illustrates is the fact that active life, living in this world with
its many demands, especially those of the body, inevitably involves
man in sin.[8] This fact calls not for shocked horror but for a consideration of how man may, in this sinful world, manage somehow to do
good. The answer is, first, that man must perform the cleansing act of
penance, to which his conscience will lead him; and second, that man
must lead (or accept) a life of patient poverty. By refusing to be too
solicitous about bodily needs and accepting patiently the condition of
poverty which will be the consequence, man will demonstrate his love
for and his faith in God, and he will lead a life which will offer great
promise of salvation. It will give him a claim on a future reward, it
will be itself a kind of penance, and it will limit the opportunities for
sin. To accept poverty is to follow the law of love: Patience tells
Haukyn that perfect charity is patient poverty. It is a difficult way of
life, but man has the virtue he needs to follow it: Patience. Haukyn's
final speech means he will follow it. Through Haukyn, then, the poet

---

7. For the references to Burdach see above, p. 32, n. 1.

8. According to Robertson and Huppé, Haukyn's sinfulness is the consequence of the
corruption of the church militant and the easy confessions of the friars: *Scriptural
Tradition*, pp. 169, 175–6. But the text itself makes no attack on the friars, and there
are several references to confession to the priest: cf. XIII.412, XIV.9.

raises the problem of moral action in this world with its demands and temptations,[9] and in the speeches of Conscience and Patience he solves it. Haukyn contrasts with the learned Doctor, who knew what men ought to do for the salvation of their souls but would not practice it himself. Haukyn, like the Doctor, was stained with the sins of the world, though his, at least, were the consequence of hard labor. Ignorant though he was, however, he listened to the voice of conscience, and with patience he could follow the way of life that would win salvation. Through Haukyn the poet asserts his conviction that sinful man can do well.

Dowel as a whole is concluded. It has dramatized the contribution to man's salvation made by the First Person of the Trinity, Kynde, God the Father and Creator. God has given man a gift which enables him to meet the terms of Piers' pardon, the injunction to do well. This gift is man's intellectual soul. Because of it man is able to know what is good and to do what is good. The process of knowing is subject to a grave fault—pride, overweening curiosity, presumptuousness—but the soul has in itself not only this weakness but its cure. By reason and "imaginatif" man can see this fault, be shamed, and correct it. The good which man knows by his intellect is the law of love, embodied specifically in the life of patient poverty. In the process of knowing the good, man's God-given intellect is assisted to some extent by the world of nature, itself created by God, which teaches him moral lessons. In the process of putting his knowledge of the good into practice, man is led by a faculty of his soul, conscience, and by the virtue of patience. These enable him to do good by leading him to perform penance and by helping him to lead the life of patient poverty, by which the law of love is fulfilled. God will assist man in this way of life by providing for his bodily needs, preoccupation with which ordinarily causes much of man's sin. Man uses these gifts falteringly, but he has them to use if he will. And so he can meet one requisite of salvation: he can do well.

9. Burdach (*Ackermann,* pp. 305–8) suggests that Haukyn is contrasted with the Learned Doctor of the Banquet Scene to show the greater piety of the unlearned. The greater piety of the unlearned is argued by the Dreamer in his clash with Clergy and Scripture (x.452–74), and a certain antagonism toward learning is perceptible in the Banquet Scene. But Imaginatif's defense of learning answers the Dreamer's attack, and the Banquet Scene shows the Dreamer reconciled with Clergy. It concludes by assigning Clergy a very useful if somewhat pedestrian role in the scheme of salvation (xiii.202–14). Burdach errs, I believe, in making it appear that the poet ultimately rejects learning. It may be part of the poet's purpose to contrast Haukyn with the Doctor, but the contrast points up the difference between the Doctor's not doing what is good although he knows it, and Haukyn's willingness to do the good when he learns what the good is. The main purpose of the scene with Haukyn, however, is to illustrate the problem of sin that is involved in the active life, and how this problem can be solved within the limits of the active life.

6

The Visions of Dobet

THE FIRST problem in *Dobet* is a problem in organization, not meaning. There is a puzzle about the relationship between *Dowel* and the opening lines of *Dobet*. The colophon clearly states that *Dowel* ends here and *Dobet* begins. But is *Dowel* really finished? The interlude in the real world that opens *Dobet* shows the Dreamer half insane because he still lacked the natural knowledge of Dowel which he had been seeking. Since Reason then puts him to sleep out of pity, the expectation is that the vision will provide this natural knowledge. In the dream Soul does discuss natural knowledge and its limitations; thereafter the subject is never raised again. Soul also delivers a long discourse on charity, a subject often referred to in *Dowel* but never treated at length. In Christian doctrine, of course, charity is the essence of the law. The friar at the opening of *Dowel* had stated that Dowel was charity, and in so saying had set in motion the quest for a natural knowledge of Dowel. Although Soul does not say Dowel is charity, it seems reasonable to assume that Soul's long explanation of charity ends the quest. The Dreamer at last achieves the natural knowledge of Dowel he sought for so long. He learns in unmistakable terms that the essence of the good life is love. Man can know this by natural knowledge, for the soul by its nature loves.[1]

The C-text supports the suggestion that Soul's speech is related to the quest in *Dowel*. In the C-text *Dowel* does not end until Soul has made a good part of his speech about charity.[2] The result is rather awkward: *Dowel* ends and *Dobet* begins in the middle of a vision and in the middle of a dialogue. Apparently the poet felt that in the B-text version he had obscured the concluding point about Dowel by placing it in *Dobet*. In the C-text version he sought to clarify the point by bringing *Dowel* to a close only after he had made the speech about charity. Or, what is less debatable, he felt he would be doing no violence to the intellectual structure of his poem by including in *Dowel* lines which originally were part of *Dobet*.[3]

1. Cf. the quotation from Bartholomaeus Anglicus, cited above, p. 46.
2. C.XVII.371; B.xv, about 252.
3. Coghill suggested that *Dobet* really begins at B.xv.144: *MedAev, 2*, 124. Donaldson concluded that "neither B nor C had any very clear idea where Do-Well left off and Do-Bet began." P. 29, n. 8.

Nothing vital hinges on this suggestion.[4] Love has been praised too often in *Dowel* for any reader not to see its importance. Here love is given a form commensurate with its importance in the poem. If it is a kind of climax to the talk of love in *Dowel*, however, this does not mean it is significant for *Dowel* alone. *Dobet* is also concerned with charity. Otherwise the speech about charity would not be there. Even in the revised C-text *Dobet*, the discussion of charity runs to several hundred lines. In both B and C charity is discussed in other parts of *Dobet* as well. In other words, the theme of charity in *Dowel* spills over into *Dobet* and provides the kind of gliding transition the poet was partial to.[5] *Dobet*, of course, treats charity from a different point of view. *Dowel* had shown that charity was the basis of the moral law and that man could know the law of love and follow it. *Dobet*, in Soul's speech, preaches that examples of men obedient to the law of love are needed to encourage other men to obey the law, and it narrates the supreme example of charity, Christ's sacrifice on the cross. The talk about the life of charity leads logically to another point, that man by his charity alone would never have won salvation. Only Christ's charity could open for mankind the gates of paradise. In *Dobet*, then, man is still urged to follow the law of love, but it is Christ's charity which is the special object of attention, as the example for man to strive to follow.

It has been obvious to all readers that the figure of Christ dominates *Dobet*, but there has been uncertainty about the significance of this fact.

4. Mensendieck felt there was no real contradiction in the poet's shifting the beginning of *Dobet* in B to the conclusion of *Dowel* in C, since Mensendieck believed that *Dobet* does not expound a way of life different from that preached in *Dowel* but gives an example of the way of life taught in *Dowel*. The change from B to C, Mensendieck believed, is a consequence of the poet's intellectual development. In B the poet had learned what Dowel was and desired to show at once a life corresponding to Dowel. So he began *Dobet* in B at an earlier point than he does in C. By the time he writes C he is more skeptical of man's abilities to lead the good life. So in C the question of the practicability of leading the good life is raised within *Dowel*, where the good life is being discussed at a theoretical level. Only then can *Dobet*, an illustration of the practical realization of the good life, follow: *Charakterentwickelung*, p. 61.

5. Cf. the way in which the issue of Dowel, which is raised in the Pardon Scene at the end of the *Visio*, slides into *Dowel*. The scene with the Learned Doctor which opens the second vision of *Dowel* blends the theme of the first vision—*knowing* what is good—with the theme of the second vision—*doing* what is good. Conscience's sermon at the opening of *Dobest* picks up the narrative of Christ's life, the content of the previous vision, and uses it to slide into the theme of the first vision of *Dobest*, the gift of grace and *redde quod debes*. The talk about the cardinal virtues by Need at the opening of the second vision of *Dobest* echoes the talk about these virtues which had closed the previous vision. A somewhat similar technique is sometimes used by the poet to move from one issue to another in a scene or speech: a word used at the conclusion of the discussion of one issue is picked up and repeated at the beginning of the discussion of the new issue. Notice how "books" is used to move from Scripture's sermon to Trajan's speech: XI.134 f.; and how "thieves" is used to move from the discussion of the value of learning to the discussion of the salvation of the wicked in Imaginatif's speech: XII.191 f.

Critics have said that Christ here illustrates the Christian life,[6] that He shows examples of the highest principles of life as these have been established in *Dowel* and also performs the work of salvation,[7] that by His act of redemption He shows the love which redeems.[8] There can be no objection to these suggestions except to their incompleteness. They point in the right direction. This cannot be said for the suggestion of Wells, Coghill, and Chambers that *Dobet* shows the Contemplative Life and that Christ is a symbol of this way of life.[9]

As I have already observed, according to medieval teaching Christ demonstrated the Contemplative Life when he "lafte þe conuersacion of al worldly men, & of his disciples also, & went alone in to desert vpon þe hulles, & contyn[u]ed al þe niȝt in preyers as þe gospel seiþ." [1] *Dobet* shows nothing like this. It shows Christ as he "comuned & medled wiþ men," living the Active Life. Another objection to the interpretation of Wells, Coghill, and Chambers is that the doctrine taught in *Dobet* cannot be so limited in its application. It applies not to a special group of men or way of life but to all men. Much of the narrative centers on the rescue of man's soul after death from the devil, the consequence of Christ's passion. To the medieval mind no action of Christ affected mankind more universally than this. The narrative in *Dobet* was, in its literal significance, so dramatic to the medieval mind that a poet could have endowed it with a symbolic value only by means of explicit statement, something that is not found in *Dobet*.

The one element that tends to support the "Contemplative theory" is the series of remarks about hermits in Soul's long speech on charity.[2] This is not evidence sufficient to prove that *Dobet* as a whole teaches the Contemplative Life. And these remarks arise, as the context shows, out of a concern with all men and their need for living examples of morality to reform them and encourage them to lead a good life. The reference to hermits of other days is a way of saying that there were men of good life to provide models of morality for mankind in the past, and there could and should be such models for mankind in the poet's day.

Another weakness of this theory and of the other explanations is their failure to explain all the major elements in *Dobet*. These are the doctrine of charity, presented in both narrative and expository form;

6. Elizabeth Deering Hanscom, "The Argument of the *Vision of Piers Plowman*," *PMLA, 9* (1894), 420.

7. Mensendieck, *Charakterentwickelung,* pp. 60–1, 64.

8. Glunz, *Literarästhetik,* pp. 534–5.

9. The references for Wells, Coghill, and Chambers have been given above, pp. 6–7, nn. 1, 2, 4, and 5.

1. Cf. "Epistle on Mixed Life," in *Yorkshire Writers, 1,* 269. Cf. also Gregory the Great, *Moralium Libri Job,* VI, 37 (PL, *75,* cols. 760–1), and XXVIII, 14 (PL, *76,* col. 467).

2. XV.263–303.

the discussion of examples of charity; the doctrine of the Trinity; and the various narrative scenes: the Tree of Charity or Patience; the coming of Christ; Abraham, Moses, and the Samaritan; and finally the Crucifixion and the Harrowing of Hell. These elements are brought into a meaningful pattern if one understands that the poet is dramatizing the contributions of Christ which further assist man to salvation. They come in this second division, *Dobet,* because they are the gift of the Second Person of the Trinity and they came second in historical time— that is, during the life of Christ on earth and after the creation of man with his rational soul.

These contributions of Christ are the reason for the title *Dobet.* The terms Dowel, Dobet, and Dobest, of course, disappear in this section. The poet apparently felt that the question of Dowel, Dobet, and Dobest was answered. They are all one—obedience to the law of love. The title *Dobet* is an indication that what is shown in this section better enables man to obey the law of love. *Dowel* showed man relying on his own resources—what his intellectual soul could give him in the way of knowledge and guidance in the struggle to do good. It was a bare "doing well" that he could aspire to. The assistance of Christ produces a greater capacity for moral action. This greater moral strength and knowledge, not a new way of life, is the poet's reason for the title *Dobet.*

The first of these gifts of Christ was the doctrine of the Trinity. As both the Apostle's Creed and the Athanasian Creed state, and as preachers and moralists loved to remind their audience, belief in the Trinity was necessary for salvation: "For þat is þe foundement of þe feiþ, to bileue in þe holi trinite." [3] Before Christ's coming, faith in the Trinity lay hidden in the faith of the learned. [4] It could not be known by reason alone, as could the law of love. [5] Christ taught the doctrine to all men so that all might know it, believe, and be saved. [6] This is still the official doctrine of the Roman Catholic Church. [7] It is for this reason that Piers Plowman, the symbol of the human nature of Christ, teaches the doctrine of the Trinity obliquely in an inner dream, and the Samaritan, the symbol of the divine nature of Christ, teaches it explicitly and at some length. It is one of the great gifts of Christ to mankind, without which man could not be saved.

The second great gift of Christ was His voluntary sacrifice on the

---

3. *Vices and Virtues,* p. 6. Cf. *Mirk's Festial: A Collection of Homilies,* ed. Theodor Erbe, EETS, e.s. *96* (London, 1905), 165; *Summa Theologica,* I, q. 32, i, ad. 3; II–II, q. 2, viii. See also *Corpus Iuris Canonici* (Basel, 1670), Decretals of Pope Gregory IX, Bk. I, title i, chaps. i–ii, pp. 1–4.
4. *Summa Theologica,* II–II, q. 2, viii.
5. Ibid., I, q. 32, i.
6. Cf. Wyclif's sermon on Trinity Sunday: *Select Wycliff, 1,* 158–62 (No. LIV).
7. G. H. Joyce, "Trinity, the Blessed," *Catholic Encyclopedia, 15,* 47.

cross and His harrowing of hell. These actions comprise a good part
of the narrative in *Dobet*. From them came two contributions to man's
salvation. First, Christ gave mankind an example of charity and patient
suffering. Preachers and theologians taught that men needed examples
of the good life to be guided and encouraged to obey the law of love.
The sufferings of the saints are beneficial to the Church, not by way of
redemption, says St. Thomas, but as examples and exhortations.[8] We
have many examples, Christ and all holy men, to teach us to avoid
sin, a fourteenth-century preacher tells his audience.[9] Christ's voluntary sacrifice was, of course, the supreme example of charity, and its
importance for mankind *as an example* was insisted on by the Bible,[1]
theologians,[2] and preachers.[3] It is for this reason that Soul speaks of
the importance of Christ's example, of the example of good men in
the past, and of the need for such examples in the poet's own day.
And this is part of the reason for the Samaritan scene and the Crucifixion scene in *Dobet*.

But the greatest gift of Christ and the one on which the poet concentrates was His redemption of mankind from the devil's power.
Adam's sin had closed heaven to mankind.[4] Tricked by the devil, man,
because of his sin, was left by God under the devil's bondage.[5] In these
circumstances Moses' law, the law of love, could not raise men from the
sin of death to the bliss of heaven.[6] All men, however obedient to the
law of love, even the patriarchs, were imprisoned in hell.[7] This is
represented in the scene where the souls of the just fall from the Tree
of Charity and are gathered up by the fiend. But Christ, by His sacrifice, vanquished death.[8a] He broke forever the devil's claim upon the
souls of the just, harrowed hell, and released the souls of the patriarchs
and the faithful. Salvation, which had been closed to mankind since
the fall of Adam, was once more attainable. For the medieval Christian,
Christ's breaking of the devil's power was the most dramatic moment
in human history. St. Augustine gave the doctrine wide circulation in
On the Trinity,[9a] later theologians repeated it,[1a] and the preachers and

8. *Summa Theologica*, III, q. 48, v, ad 3.
9. *Sermons*, p. 146. The importance of examples was one reason why evil-living
priests and prelates were attacked: p. 53.
1. I Peter ii: 21.
2. *Summa Theologica*, III, q. 46, iii; q. 49, i.
3. *Vices and Virtues*, pp. 112–13; *Select Wyclif, 1*, 31–2, 129–30.
4. *Summa Theologica*, III, q. 49, v.
5. Ibid., III, q. 46, iii, obj. 3 and ad 3; q. 48, iv, ad 2.
6. Cf. *Sermons*, p. 172.
7. Ibid., pp. 171–2; *Summa Theologica*, III, q. 49, ii. Burdach, *Ackermann*, pp. 318–
19, has some interesting material on the devil's right to man's soul before the death
of Christ.
8a. *Summa Theologica*, III, q. 46, xi, ad 1; q. 47, ii; q. 48, i.
9a. NP-N, *3*, 175–8 (Bk. XIII, chaps. 12–15).
1a. In addition to the *Summa Theologica*, cited several times above, see Petrus
Lombardus, *Sententiarum Libri Quatuor*, Sent. III, dist. 19 (PL, *192*, cols. 795–8).

moralists constantly reminded their fellow men that Christ "losed vs owte of þe þraldam of þe fende." [2] It was, of course, a popular theme in medieval art. The dramatic success of the poet's treatment of the most exacting theme in the entire poem is proof positive that he was a great artist.

The interpretation offered here accounts for all the elements in *Dobet*. After Soul's speech every scene dramatizes one or another of Christ's contributions to man's salvation. And Christ's example of charity runs through much of Soul's lengthy sermon. Soul's concern for the conversion of the heathen [3] is perhaps the one element not directly related to Christ. The poet wanders from his theme here, but it is not difficult to see how he wandered. About to tell of the gifts of Christ, by which the way to salvation was opened to mankind, he thinks of those denied this chance for eternity, the heathen. Only the failure of men in the Church to do their duty, only the corruption of priests and prelates by the arch-enemy of the law of love, money and riches, bars the way for the heathen to learn and accept the true faith. The poet grieves to see that whereas Christ died that all men might be saved, prelates and priests will not do their simple duty and make His gift available to all. Some such association as this, I believe, connects the conversion speech of Soul with the main theme of *Dobet*.

The talk about Dowel in the interlude [4] seems intended to prepare for the definition of charity by Soul which gives the Dreamer at last his "kynde knowynge" of Dowel. Perhaps his strange behavior and irreverence for the rich emphasize his intense desire to know the good.[5] In the dream which Reason mercifully sends him, the Dreamer meets Soul. Soul synthesizes both strands of *Dowel*. The soul contains man's whole moral power, both the faculties of knowing and the faculties which guide his moral actions. But more important, the soul enables man to fulfill the law of love. By the soul man naturally loves. In the soul, says Alcuin, "est amor naturaliter, quia amor intellectu discernendus est, et ratione ab illicitis delectationibus [cohibendus] [sic], ut ea amet quae amanda sunt." [6] One of the names for the soul is love:

> And whan I loue lelly · owre lorde and alle other,
> Thanne is lele Loue my name · and in Latyn *Amor*. . . .[7]

Soul is the logical character to expound the law of love to man, for it is by virtue of his soul that man is able to love God and his neighbor. The first vision of *Dobet* will close with the Samaritan, the symbol of

2. *Sermons*, p. 171.
3. xv.530–601.
4. xv.1–11.
5. On the possibly autobiographical significance of this and similar passages, see Donaldson, pp. 151-2.
6. *De Animae Ratione*, PL, *101*, col. 644.
7. xv.33-4.

Christ and His charity, telling the Dreamer of the importance of love and advising him that all men have the power to love:

> For vnkyndenesse is the contrarie · of alkynnes resoun;
> For there nys syke ne sori · ne non so moche wrecche,
> That he ne may louye, and hym lyke · and lene of his herte
> Good wille and good worde · bothe wisshen and willen
> Alle manere men · mercy and forȝifnesse,
> And louye hem liche hym-self · and his lyf amende.[8]

Man can obey the law of charity—because he has a soul. Soul here tells the Dreamer of charity.

Soul's long speech [9] on charity and kindred matters contains a rebuke to the Dreamer much like Imaginatif's. It is a rebuke for his desire to know all things. This is pride. What is needful is that man should turn his knowledge into good works. Soul then attacks at great length those who know what charity is but do not practice it, especially priests and friars. They should be examples of goodness to men but are corrupted by the antithesis of morality and the law of love, money.[1]

The second part of Soul's speech, the definition of charity,[2] is not a technical, theological definition so much as a rhetorical description, an effort to breathe life into a concept. The effort is successful. Details from St. Paul's description of charity mingle with images from the poet's own imagination to produce a picture bright and joyous in tone.

---

8. XVII.343–8.

9. In the C-text, Soul or Anima is called Liberum Arbitrium. This change probably does not imply any doctrine about the soul or about charity which is radically different from that in B. George Sanderlin has shown that John Damascene and some other theologians considered *liberum arbitrium* a universal power of the soul, containing its whole nature, and therefore synonymous with the soul: "The Character 'Liberum Arbitrium' in the C-text of *Piers Plowman*," *MLN, 56* (1941), 449–53, esp. 450–1. By changing the name of Soul to Liberum Arbitrium in C, the poet has simply emphasized the fact that man has the power to obey the law of love if he will—the same point that is made in the speech of the Samaritan quoted above (a passage which C retains without any change: C.xx.325–30). Donaldson has a detailed discussion of the substitution of Liberum Arbitrium for Anima and Piers in *Dobet:* pp. 180–95. Of particular interest is his conclusion that "on the matter of the almost unlimited importance of Liberum Arbitrium, B and C are in accord, despite C's drastic revision" (p. 192). Donaldson also points out that B emphasizes the fact that the will is the emotional faculty, the faculty capable of experiencing love. The C-poet, he believes, "desirous of emphasizing charity to the utmost, took the hint from B to make Liberum Arbitrium, the emotional faculty of the soul, serve as the prologue to a dramatization of charity" (p. 193).

1. This philosophy had been established, of course, in the very first vision of the poem. The Dreamer had inquired about the nature of Wrong, the evil force in the world; Holy Church had told him that money and the law of love were polar opposites (II.29–38); as a specific answer to his inquiry she had shown him the drama of Lady Meed.

2. XV.145–252.

Charity is like a child[3] but not childish,[4] says Soul. He follows the way of life which Patience recommended to Haukyn (*ne solliciti sitis,* patient poverty), for charity does not worry about his food. He relies on *fiat voluntas tua* and *spera in deo* and cleanses himself with penance, especially contrition. Only Piers Plowman knows the man who has true charity, for clerks can see only words and works, which may be misleading.[5] He may be found among rich and poor. The food he lives on is God's passion; he neither begs nor borrows. No matter what men suffer, says Soul, they should never lose the spirit of charity, for they should remember that Christ suffered more. And He did this, not out of necessity,

> Ac he suffred in ensample · that we shulde suffre also,
> And seide to suche that suffre wolde · that *pacientes vincunt.*[6]

This reference to the example of Christ's charity leads to the lengthy discussion of the effect which good men, by their example, have on others.[7] For all the asides in the speech, there is a dominating idea: mankind needs examples of good men in the Church whose lives are ruled by charity. The Church, however, is corrupted by riches and cupidity. If the Church and the clergy would reform, a golden age would dawn. By their example they would reform all Christians of evil life and convert the heathen to the true faith. Such is the power of good examples.

When the speech is ended, the Dreamer thanks Soul for the love of Haukyn the Active Man. (This remark would be meaningless if Dobet were devoted to contemplatives or clerks, since it certainly means that Soul's teaching is directed at the active man.) And then the poem returns abruptly to the subject of charity. The Dreamer says he is still puzzled about the meaning of charity. Soul responds with the

---

3. Quoting, at xv.145, from Matthew xviii: 3: "Nisi efficiamini sicut paruuli, non intrabitis in regnum celorum."

4. An echo, I assume, of I Corinthians xiii: 11.

5. xv.189–208. This passage is altered in C to make what appears to be one of the most complete reversals of opinion in the two texts. "Do not clerks know charity?" asks the Dreamer. Liberum Arbitrium replies that Piers Plowman knows him most perfectly. You will never know charity by clothing or by talk. "'Ac thorw werkes thou myght wite wher forth he walketh; *Operibus credite'*" (C.xvii.339). Donaldson, pp. 194–5, discussing the alteration, thinks C is merely improving B's logic, for elsewhere B supports the doctrine of good works. I would suggest that the reversal is not so complete as it seems. In B as well as in C the poet believes that true charity must lead to the performance of good works; he has, in fact, just finished enumerating some of the good works that charity performs. But in B he emphasizes the point that what looks like a charitable work may be only a hypocritical gesture. In C his skepticism is not so marked. Through works you *might* know where charity is, says Liberum Arbitrium. In both versions the poet believes in good works as the basis of morality.

6. xv.261–2.

7. xv.263–601.

metaphor of the Tree of Charity or Patience.[8] The tree metaphor is a convenient device for expounding quickly a number of moral lessons —the importance of mercy, of the creed, and of patience. The tree is called patience and poor in heart. Through God and good men it grows its fruit, charity. It grows in man's heart and is cared for by Liberum Arbitrium. This is familiar doctrine, already taught in *Dowel:* man has the power to do deeds of charity (obey the law of love) if he wills. What is about to be shown, however, is that good works will not in themselves win salvation for man.

The inner dream occurs when the Dreamer swoons with joy at hearing the name of Piers Plowman, who has entrusted the tree and garden to Liberum Arbitrium. The inner dream in *Dobet* does not serve so clear a function as the inner dream in *Dowel.* The dream within a dream there came when the progress of the narrative had been brought to a complete halt by the Dreamer's skepticism. There the inner dream translated the action to a different level and prepared for the solution of the Dreamer's doubts. The inner dream in *Dobet* seems a mechanical repetition of a novel device. The poet of the C-text was apparently aware of this, for he dropped the inner dream from *Dobet.* Nothing is lost by the omission. The probable purpose of the brief inner vision is to present in narrative form the fact that man could not be saved without certain gifts from Christ dramatized in later passus of *Dobet:* Christ's teaching and example of the law of love, His teaching of the doctrine of the Trinity, and His freeing of mankind from the devil's power.[9]

The mystery of the doctrine of the Trinity is introduced in the inner dream when Piers explains to the Dreamer that the three props of the

8. XVI.1–17. The tree image is a commonplace in medieval writing. To some extent it probably is inspired by the numerous tree images in the Bible: the tree of life and the tree of the knowledge of good and evil in Genesis ii: 9, the tree of the rivers of water in Psalm 1: 3, the tree of life in Revelations xxii: 2, etc. To establish the specific source of the image in a late medieval writer is virtually impossible. As Donaldson remarks, "The history of trees in religious allegory seems very complex" (p. 183, n. 1). He refers to Burdach, *Ackermann,* pp. 285–7, and p. 285, n. 2. For this reason, and for the reason that no very close correspondence is revealed, Miss Mabel Day's argument that the tree image in this scene comes from Duns Scotus is unconvincing: "Duns Scotus and 'Piers Plowman,'" *RES, 3* (1927), 333–4. Robertson and Huppé, *Scriptural Tradition,* pp. 191–2, discuss the tree, but in a review of their book in *Speculum, 27* (1952), 246–7, Morton Bloomfield states that they confuse the concept of the trees of virtues and vices with the *Lignum Vitae* and the tree of charity, "the genera to which the tree in Passus XVI certainly belongs." There is a strikingly similar tree image in *Vices and Virtues,* pp. 93–6, 114.

9. Donaldson has a detailed discussion of the scene in *Piers Plowman,* pp. 183–92. The explanation which he finds most satisfactory (pp. 186–7, and n. 8, p. 186) is based on the suggestion advanced independently by Burdach (*Ackermann,* p. 228) and Dorothy Owen (*Piers Plowman: A Comparison with Some Earlier and Contemporary French Allegories,* London, 1912, pp. 123–4) that the scene is a "single allegory dealing with the pre-Christian era." The suggestion might explain why the poet resorted to the device of the dream within a dream: it enabled him to make this abrupt, backward jump in time to the pre-Christian era.

Tree of Charity are the Three Persons of the Trinity, who protect the fruit of the Tree. (In the inner dream, the fruit is both acts of charity and the souls of the just who have done such acts.) God, the power of the Father, protects the fruit from the world and its covetousness. The Son, the wisdom of the Father, protects the fruit from the flesh and its lusts. Liberum Arbitrium sometimes allows the devil to steal fruit, i.e. man sins of his own free will, and deliberate sin is sin against the Holy Ghost. But when the world, the flesh, and the devil all threaten the fruit, Liberum Arbitrium drives them away with the help of the Holy Ghost, the Third Person of the Trinity.[1]

The passage is a confusing one. The confusion arises, I believe, because the poet has tried to say two things at the same time and has not worked out a device for saying both things clearly. He is saying that man has free will, is free to sin or not sin, and that man is assisted in the fight against sin by the Three Persons of the Trinity.[2] Taken at face value, however, the passage says that free will is associated only with grace and the Holy Ghost. And the Holy Ghost does not fight the devil, the third member of the evil triad, as the logic of the image would lead one to expect, but fights only when the world, the flesh, and the devil combine to attack man. This is rather strange doctrine. It appears, I think, only because the poet has not solved the problem of expressing simultaneously two ideas, that man has free will and that he is assisted by the Trinity.

With the help of the Trinity, man can do good deeds. But man's good deeds alone will not win salvation. This is the meaning of the scene in which the devil carries off to hell the fruit (the souls of the just)[3] which Piers shakes from the tree. The inner vision concludes with the announcement that the souls of the just will be rescued and with a summary narrative of Jesus' life up to the moment of His imprisonment.[4] In the biography, the healing miracles are stressed.[5] The

1. In the C-text the Father protects against the world, the Son against the flesh, and the Holy Ghost against the devil. Liberum Arbitrium is associated with all three actions: C.xix.25–52; cf. B.xvi.23–52. I agree with Donaldson that the incident is more intelligible in C than in B: pp. 187–8, and on the orthodoxy of the view expressed in C's revision see p. 187, n. 4. On the role played by Liberum Arbitrium in C and the doctrinal significance of this, see Donaldson, pp. 188–93, and Sanderlin, *MLN, 56,* 449–53.

2. In the scene we get a glimpse, I believe, of the poet's concept of man doing well, better, and best and winning salvation with the help of the Trinity, the concept which provides, I am arguing, the over-all scheme of *Dowel, Dobet, and Dobest.*

3. The fruit on the tree is divided into the three ways of life, marriage, widowhood, and virginity (xvi.64–72). They show that all souls were claimed by the devil until the sacrifice of Christ. The triad also echoes, however, the Trinity theme which runs through this first vision of *Dobet*. Cf. the triad Faith, Hope, and Charity later in the vision.

4. xvi.90–159.

5. Although the healing miracles may have been recounted for their own sake, they may have an allegorical value also. St. Thomas Aquinas mentions the doctrine that

inner vision is a prologue and a preparation for the Crucifixion and the Harrowing of Hell.

Greatly excited by this crisis in the drama of salvation, the Dreamer awakens and seeks for Piers. He wakens, presumably, into the original vision, but the characters he now meets—Faith (Abraham), Hope (Moses), and the Samaritan (Charity and the divine nature of Christ) —are unrelated to Anima or Soul, the character in the first part of this vision. In *Dowel* Imaginatif was clearly related to Wit, Study, *et al.*, who had appeared before the interrupting dream, for they all were part of the process of knowing. The relation between the two portions of the dream in *Dobet* is not a relation between characters but between doctrines. Soul expounds the law of love, and so does Hope. Moreover, the law of love is fulfilled symbolically in the action of the Samaritan. Soul urges that men need examples of love; the Samaritan incident is such an example and symbolically represents the greatest example, Christ's redemption of mankind. The man of charity, Soul's concern, needs the charity of Christ, the principal theme of the Faith-Hope-Samaritan sequence.

This sequence does more than teach that Christ's charity was essential for man's salvation: because of His love for mankind Christ sac.ificed Himself on the cross to redeem man from the devil's power and taught man the doctrine of the Trinity, which he needed to know in order to be saved. In the process of representing this doctrine the scene also teaches that there are faith, hope, and charity, these three, but the greatest of these is charity.[6] Faith in the scene is faith in the coming of Christ to release the souls of the just. Hope is hope of rescue by Christ. The Samaritan scene represents the fulfillment of this faith, the realization of this hope, by charity. Christ's charity, His sacrifice, releases the souls of the just. Faith also teaches a doctrine based on faith, the doctrine of the Trinity as it was obscurely hinted at, according to the commentators, in the Old Testament; and Hope teaches a doctrine based on hope, the doctrine of love. The Samaritan, Charity, teaches explicitly the doctrine of the Trinity and the doctrine of love. The role played by the Samaritan in the scene reveals that "the greatest of these is charity."

---

the healing miracles signify the healing of spiritual diseases, whereby men are delivered from sin: *Summa Theologica*, III, q. 84, x, obj. 3.

6. For a disquisition on the theological virtues see the *Summa Theologica*, I–II, q. 62, and, on a humbler level, *Vices and Virtues*, pp. 121–2. Faith precedes hope and hope precedes charity in the conventional sequence of the theological virtues, not only because charity is the greatest of these three but also because man must have faith before he can have hope and he must have hope before he can have charity. Whether the poet intended this significance to attach to his use of the conventional order would be difficult to say.

In the scene the Dreamer first meets Faith or Abraham,[7] a conventional symbol of faith,[8] pertinent here because Abraham expounds the doctrine of the Trinity, a matter of faith, and he represents those who had faith in the coming of Christ and His release of the souls of the just from hell. Next the Dreamer meets Spes or Hope, identified with Moses.[9] Hope is waiting for Christ, by His sacrifice, to fulfill the law of love given on Mt. Sinai: "Dilige deum et proximum tuum," which has been glossed "In hijs duobus mandatis tota lex pendet et prophetia." By this law, Hope says, thousands have been saved. The Dreamer is puzzled as to which law he should believe. The doctrine of the Trinity which Abraham teaches has saved many, and so has this law of love, which does not mention the Trinity. Neither law is easy to obey, but of the two, Hope's law is the more difficult.

As they argue this matter, they see a Samaritan riding to a joust in Jerusalem. There follows a dramatization of the parable of the Good Samaritan,[1] in which Faith and Hope play the roles of the priest and the Levite, and the Samaritan helps the wounded man. The Samaritan then rides on to Jerusalem, pursued by Faith and Hope, and by the Dreamer, who questions him about the significance of this scene.[2] The familiar parable of the Samaritan teaches the doctrine of love most effectively, and that is one reason why the story is told. But that is not the only reason. The Samaritan's speech reveals that the narrative was also a symbol allegory representing Christ's rescue of the soul of mankind from the devil's power. The poem has been working toward this doctrine in the inner dream and in the speeches of Faith and Hope. In turning the parable of the Samaritan to this purpose the poet was following a traditional interpretation of the story.

According to the biblical commentators, the parable taught the law of love, but it was also a symbol allegory. The man who fell among thieves is Adam and all mankind. The thieves are the devil and his cohorts, who rob mankind of his grace and so of salvation. The priest and the Levite (Faith and Hope in this version) who pass by the wounded man are variously interpreted. Sometimes they represent Aaron, the high priest, who could not assist man to salvation by his sacrifices, and Moses, who could not help man by the Law. Sometimes they represent the time of the Law and the time of the Prophets, when man could not be saved. The Samaritan is interpreted as Christ and his beast as man's flesh (even as the poem says) in which He

7. XVI.167–271.
8. Abraham is spoken of as the man of faith in Galatians iii: 6–9, John viii: 56. Cf. *Summa Theologica*, II–II, q. I, iii.
9. XVI.272–XVII.46.
1. XVII.47–79.
2. XVII.80–123.

comes to help mankind. His care for the wounded man represents His helping mankind to salvation. Though he adds touches of his own, the poet has followed tradition in his interpretation of the parable.[3] Thus he has been able not merely to teach the importance of love but also to develop his theme, the gifts of Christ: His example of charity and His freeing of mankind from the devil.[4]

The poem now proceeds to another gift of Christ, His revelation to mankind of the doctrine of the Trinity, which man must believe to be saved. The Dreamer asks which doctrine he should follow, Faith's teaching about the Trinity or Hope's doctrine of love. The Samaritan's reply is a long sermon on the Trinity, using a series of analogies in an attempt to make the doctrine clear. First he compares the Father, Son, and Holy Ghost to the fist, fingers, and palm of the hand. These, like the Trinity, constitute three separate parts yet have a unity. The function of each part is compared to the function of the person of the Trinity which it symbolizes. And by the fact that a wound in the palm incapacitates the whole hand he illustrates the doctrine that a sin against the Holy Ghost is the most grievous of sins and quenches God's grace.[5]

Then he proceeds to another analogy, in which the persons of the Trinity are compared to the wax, wick, and fire of a candle, which together make a flame. This analogy he uses to illustrate another teaching: the law of love, and the essential unity between this doctrine and

---

3. See the *Catena Aurea*, IV, 371–7. The two sermons on the Samaritan story referred to by Skeat in *Parallel Texts, 2*, 242, follow this interpretation and give some idea of how commonplace this allegorization was. See *Select Wycliff, 1*, 31–3, and *Old English Homilies*, Ser. 1, ed. Richard Morris, EETS, o.s. *29* (London, 1868), 78–85. Robertson and Huppé, *Scriptural Tradition*, p. 198 and n. 42, quote from St. Augustine, *Quaestionum Evangeliorum*, PL, *35*, col. 1340, and the *Glossa Ordinaria*, PL, *114*, cols. 286–7. One more evidence of how widespread the interpretation was is its appearance in *The Miroure of Mans Saluacionne*, a fifteenth-century translation of the *Speculum humanae salvationis*, ed. Alfred Henry Huth, Roxburghe Club, *118* (London, 1888), 18–19.

4. There are several obscure points in the speech, although they do not involve the main theme. The Samaritan symbolizes Christ, but he says (XVII.122–3) that the babe is born in Bethlehem who shall save all men with his blood. This does not mean that the Samaritan cannot be Christ. The world of allegory is simply not consistently logical. At XVII.112–21 the Samaritan says that *after* he has chained the devil, Faith and Hope will help the souls of men " 'Tyl I haue salue for alle syke and thanne shal I retourne, And come a3ein bi this contree and confort alle syke That craueth it or coueiteth it and cryeth there-after.' " Robertson and Huppé explain part of the passage as follows: "After the Redemption, Faith has the power to teach the imitation of Christ, not simply to herald his coming. He can thus direct the pilgrim on the proper road to Jerusalem since Charity has become manifest. When the pilgrim strays from the road because he is weak in Faith, he may be restored through Hope, that is, trust in God's Charity, which will lead him to works of satisfaction under the new law" (p. 207). But what is the meaning of the salve and the promise to return? The salve of grace, bestowed on mankind after the Ascension? Or is it, as seems more likely, a reference to the Second Coming and the Day of Judgment? Cf. the words of Christ at the end of the Harrowing of Hell: XVIII.365–97.

5. XVII.131–202.

the doctrine of the Trinity. The law which Faith preached and the law which Hope preached are shown to be not contrary or separate teachings but two sides to one coin. Had not the Samaritan told the Dreamer to obey them both? The gist of his argument is this: He has already proved that the sin against the Holy Ghost is the gravest of sins. What is this sin? It is, his analogy asserts, to disobey the law of love. So the two doctrines intertwine like the red rose and the briar. Belief in the Trinity, involving as it does the doctrine that the sin against the Holy Ghost is the worst of sins, leads man to obey the law of love, for not to obey it is to sin against the Holy Ghost.[6]

The analogy by which this point is established is not always easy to follow, because it is not always consistent, but in outline it is this. The Father, Son, and Holy Ghost are like the wax, wick, and fire of a candle. Together they produce a flame, love and belief, which cleanses Christians of sins. (This seems to be the state of grace.) Men who disobey the law of love sin against the Holy Ghost and so blow out this fire. Though the wick (the Son) still smoulders, i.e. though only the fire is quenched (only the Holy Ghost is sinned against), there is no flame (no forgiveness of sins, no grace). Only when the Holy Ghost, fanned by love (obedience to the law of love) blazes up is there flame (forgiveness of sins). So long as the Holy Ghost is not sinned against there may be mercy, even as a piece of wax alone (the Father, the Son having been sinned against) or a wick alone (the Son, the Father having been sinned against) produces flame (that is, there can still be forgiveness of sins, grace) when placed in a fire (the Holy Ghost not having been sinned against). But even as one cannot produce flame from a flint without tinder, so the Holy Ghost will not grant mercy to the unkind (those who disobey the law of love, particularly rich men and murderers).[7] The merciless will never be forgiven. A man who had sinned against the Holy Ghost but had repented, confessed,

6. XVII.203–92. St. Thomas Aquinas distinguishes three meanings which had been given to the sin against the Holy Ghost: the earlier doctors had said that it was to utter a blasphemy against the Holy Spirit; St. Augustine had said it was final impenitence; others, including St. Thomas himself, apparently believed it was to sin through certain malice, through the very choosing of evil: *Summa Theologica*, II-II, q. 14, i. He distinguished six kinds of sin against the Holy Ghost: despair, presumption, impenitence, obstinacy, resisting the known truth, and envy of our brother's spiritual good: II-II, q. 14, ii. Because of this uncertainty as to the exact nature of the sin, it is difficult to say whether the poet was unorthodox or not in his description of the sin. He seems to have reasoned that, since the Holy Ghost was the charity of the Father and the Son, lack of charity in man was the sin against the Holy Ghost.

7. XVII.250–92. Penances, pilgrimages, and indulgences, he warns, will be of no avail. The rich are advised to remember the fate of Dives. This is the recurrent theme of the antithesis between money and the law of love. Murderers are worse, for they quench the light of a man's life. Here the symbolic value of light changes, but the double value of the symbol is apparently used to reinforce the contention that to quench the light is both murder and the sin against the Holy Ghost.

and cried on God for mercy might be saved, but it is unlikely. All things
are possible for God, for He is all-powerful and His mercy is greater
than all our wicked works. Such sinners, however, usually do not repent
but instead fall into despair, which drives away grace.[8]

The Samaritan concludes his speech and the vision by saying that
sins of the flesh are easily forgiven the man who asks for mercy and
tries to amend, and impatience at the sorrows of life is forgiven. But
unkindness " 'quencheth goddes mercy.' " For unkindness is against
reason. There is no man so wretched that he cannot love his neighbor
as himself and obey the law of love.[9]

By linking the law of love with the Trinity and by asserting that
disobedience to this law is a sin against the Holy Ghost, the Samaritan
has given powerful support to the doctrine of charity. The vision ends
as it began, with a discussion of love. It has shown what the soul of
man tells him about charity and what Christ (the Samaritan) tells him.
Quite properly, Christ's message is more positive and more dramatic.
What Soul could tell man could not compare in power or authority
to what Christ revealed. Christ taught man that the whole law was
contained in the commandment to love God and one's neighbor. And
He taught that unless this command was obeyed, one could not be
saved. This is the Samaritan's message in *Dobet*.

The vision has also shown Christ, first as Piers, the symbol of the
human nature of Christ, then as the Samaritan, the symbol of His
divine nature, revealing to mankind the doctrine of the Trinity. Man's
reason alone could not discover this doctrine, yet it must be believed
if man is to be saved. Finally, the vision has reminded the reader that
the charity of man could never have won salvation by its own merit,
for mankind lacked grace and the souls of men were forfeit to the
devil. Only the charity of Christ could free them. The next vision will
tell the story of this liberation.

The second vision of *Dobet* is a literal narrative. It is told because
of its dramatic power and its significance, but that significance is not
hidden. The narrative does not shadow forth a concealed meaning.
The poet is telling of the Crucifixion of Christ and the Harrowing of
Hell, when by His sacrifice Christ redeemed men's souls from the devil
and made salvation possible in spite of the sins of Adam. The narrative has no more meaning than this. It could hardly have had any
other for the medieval mind. That was meaning enough.

The picture in the interlude of a distracted man, so similar to the
sketches of the Dreamer at the beginning of *Dobet* and at his awakening
from the inner dream, may be intended to suggest the state of man before the Crucifixion had re-opened the way to salvation. Aesthetically
the scene is most effective, for it heightens by contrast the joy of the

8. XVII.293–314.
9. XVII.315–50.

Dreamer when he awakens after the Harrowing of Hell. To create that contrast is probably the purpose of the interlude.[1]

The vision opens with a procession through city streets on Palm Sunday.[2] One who looks like both Piers and the Samaritan is riding to joust against the fiend. (The human and divine nature of Christ are joined here, as they were during His life on earth.) The familiar medieval Christ-knight image [3] has been used to announce the coming struggle in hell, and for a moment the poem recreates the excitement in London streets on the day of a tourney. The same realism characterizes the scene of the trial and Crucifixion.[4] Particularly striking is its brevity and concentration. A few shrill cries and accusations from the crowd, a detail or two of the torture, a glimpse of the dying Christ, and the scene is ended. The swiftness and sureness with which the short passage creates vivid images and intense emotion make it one of the great crucifixion scenes in literature. The purpose of the scene after Christ's death, with its emphasis on the tricking of the blind knight Longeus, apparently was to arouse emotion to an even greater pitch.

The debate which follows between the Four Daughters of God— Mercy, Truth, Righteousness, and Peace [5]—was a popular theme in narrative and drama from the twelfth century through the fifteenth and even later.[6] It is employed here, however, in a most original manner. Conventionally, the debate occurs at the time of the creation of man, the time of the Fall, or, most frequently, the time of the Incarnation.[7] Placing the debate just before the Harrowing of Hell was apparently the poet's own inspiration. It is a remarkably effective innovation. The debate, interrupting the narrative, creates suspense and heightens anticipation for the scene in hell which the audience would be expecting. The debate has its doctrinal purpose also, for it teaches that, judged by a code of righteousness and truth, mankind deserved to suffer in hell eternally. Only considerations of mercy and peace can urge his redemption.[8] Only the death of Christ could save mankind and at the

1. XVIII.1–5.

2. XVIII.6–35. On the probable order of lines 5–9 in XVIII see Elsie Blackman, "Notes on the B-Text MSS. of *Piers Plowman*," *JEGP*, 17 (1918), 542. For a provisional draft of the revised B-text, XVIII.1–39, see ibid., pp. 542–5.

3. See Wilbur Gaffney, "The Allegory of the Christ-Knight in *Piers Plowman*," *PMLA*, 46 (1931), 155–68; and Sister Marie de Lourdes le May, *The Allegory of the Christ-Knight in English Literature* (Washington, D.C., 1932), *passim*, but esp. pp. 31–52. Cf. the use of the theme in *Sermons*, pp. 37–8, and *The Miroure of Mans Saluacionne*, p. 135.

4. XVIII.36–109.

5. XVIII.110–259.

6. Hope Traver, *The Four Daughters of God*, Bryn Mawr College Monographs, Monograph Series, 6 (Philadelphia, 1907), *passim*. For bibliography see pp. 5–6 and nn. 1–11.

7. Traver, pp. 164–5. The theme in *Piers Plowman* is discussed on pp. 147–52.

8. Cf. the exemplum told in *Sermons*, pp. 43–5, in which Righteousness and Truth are unable to release Adam, but Mercy can.

same time reconcile the claims of truth and righteousness with those of mercy and peace.

The Harrowing of Hell is a brilliant dramatic scene: against the vivid picture of confusion, bickering, and despair among the demons is poised the monumental speech of Christ in Hell. Christ here is a blaze of light and a thundering voice. He indicts Satan for winning the soul of man by guile. For the souls of worthy men released from Satan's power, Christ offers His soul. On Doomsday, He prophesies, He will take all souls out of Hell, will reward the good, and punish the wicked. But His mercy is stressed, and the poet almost says that all men will be pardoned. It is the example of Christ's charity that the poet is preaching, not His wrath. He leads the chosen souls from Hell, and the vision closes with rejoicing as Truth and Peace embrace, Righteousness and Mercy kiss. The Dreamer, awakening to the sound of Easter bells, bids his wife and daughter kiss the cross, for God's body has rescued man from the fiend.[9]

On this note of triumph *Dobet* ends. It has shown the gifts of Christ requisite for salvation. Critics have wondered why the climax comes so long before the poem ends. The ecstatic finale of *Dobet* does contrast with the tears and repentance of Haukyn at the close of *Dowel,* the disasters and new pilgrimage which conclude *Dobest* and the whole poem. But the ending of *Dobet* is the climax of the poem only if triumph and climax are synonymous. The triumph of *Dobet* is a hymn of thanksgiving for Christ and a song of hope for mankind. Nothing man could do would threaten Christ's redemption of man from the devil's power. And the brotherhood of God and man is made flesh and blood in the figure of Christ. This is the basis of the poet's hope for mankind's salvation, the mystic faith embodied in the symbolic figure of Piers. Through the figure of Piers this hope and faith have appeared in *Dobet* again and again. In the scene in Hell Christ has promised

> . . . to be merciable to man · thanne my kynde it asketh;
> For we beth bretheren of blode. . . .
> And my mercy shal be shewed · to manye of my bretheren.
> For blode may suffre blode · bothe hungry and akale,
> Ac blode may nouȝt se blode · blede, but hym rewe.[1]

Hence the triumph of *Dobet*. But the scheme of salvation is not complete, and the poet proceeds to *Dobest*.

9. XVIII.260–431.
1. XVIII.373–4, 391–3.

7

The Visions of Dobest

TO THE casual reader *Dobest* is not so difficult as *Dowel* or *Dobet*. There are few purely doctrinal passages, and there is a great deal of action, some of it as exciting as anything in the poem. But if one goes beyond the surface of the narrative, the illusion of simplicity vanishes. Theories about *Piers Plowman* are most likely to come a cropper in *Dobest*.

The suggestion, for example, that the poem develops the Purgative, Illuminative, and Unitive stages of mystical contemplation [1] falls down badly here. Howard Meroney believes the Unitive stage begins when *Dobest* is almost finished: "I cam to Vnite . . ." says the Dreamer. But Unity is obviously the company of the faithful, the state of grace, not a state of mind. And the siege of Unity and its betrayal by the friars can hardly be the poet's dramatization of the contemplative union with God attained to in the Unitive stage. The story here is one of disunity, war, treachery, and near despair.

The theory of Wells, Coghill, and Chambers is likewise embarrassed by the actual content of *Dobest*. According to Chambers, *"Dobest . . . is the life of a spiritual leader, an ideal bishop who, from the life of poverty and contemplation, returns to active life, to guide and correct others."* [2] Wells himself remarks, however, that "in this section very little is said of bishops, less indeed than in several other parts of the poem." [3] Actually, no bishop appears, there is no discussion of an ec-

---

1. Meroney, *ELH, 17,* 8–12. See also Donaldson, pp. 158–60; but Donaldson comments, p. 197: "As it stands, Do-Best does not seem to contain much that is suggestive of the vision of God of St. Bernard."

2. *Poets and their Critics,* p. 14.

3. "The Philosophy of Piers Plowman," *PMLA, 53* (1938), 347. Wells prefers to speak of Dobest as a state of mind rather than as a sociological status: 346–9. Some other suggestions about *Dobest* might be noted here. Hanscom identified *Dobest* as the ideal life of the Church: *PMLA, 9,* 421. Mensendieck's view is that *Dobest* dramatizes the founding of the Church and the Christian community. Dobest is the perfection of good on earth according to the example of the life of Christ (Dowel) and through the strength of Christ's work of salvation (Dobet): *Charakterentwickelung,* p. 64. Burdach explains *Dobest* as concerned with the salvation of the world, lying in sin because the Church has been corrupted: *Ackermann,* pp. 313–14. For Glunz, *Dobest* (i.e. XIX.331–XX.384) reflects the evangelical prophesying about Doomsday; in it the redemption of mankind at the end of world history is not shown, for it is still awaited: *Literarästhetik,* pp. 534–5.

clesiastic's duties, and the personifications are not aspects of the episcopal office.

The elements which are stressed by discussion or personification are
these: in the first vision of *Dobest,* conscience, the doctrine of *redde
quod debes,* the Holy Paraclete or grace, the gifts of labor, the four
cardinal virtues, Unitas, contrition and confession, and the taking of
the eucharist; in the second vision, conscience, the friars, Antichrist,
need, Unitas, contrition, and grace. A valid interpretation of *Dobest*
must explain why these elements are stressed, and it must disclose the
pattern of their relationship.

The explanation I am advancing interprets *Dobest* as based doctrinally on the gifts to mankind of the Third Person of the Trinity, the
Holy Spirit, by which the scheme of salvation was completed and eternal
life made attainable by man. These gifts were the gift of grace and certain accompanying gifts.

The historical *mise-en-scène* of *Dobest* is the period immediately
after the Resurrection, and the fourteenth century. The poet dramatizes
the granting of grace by the Holy Spirit, and then turns to his own age
to examine its use of this gift. In the second vision of *Dobest,* the final
vision of the poem, the world shown is as real and as contemporary as
the field of folk with which the poem opened. Now, however, the world
is no longer portrayed as by an observer ignorant of the true meaning
of what he sees, reporting only the appearance of things, the noisy
coming and going of a confused crowd. Now the world is viewed by
one who has witnessed and understood God's scheme of salvation for
mankind, and who sees the field of folk as in fact a vast battleground
for the souls of men.[4]

Some understanding of the principal assumptions about the doctrine
of grace is a prerequisite for an intelligible reading of *Dobest.*[5] According to the doctrine, man's nature is such that, unassisted, he cannot be
saved. The possession of an intellectual soul, God's image in man, the
gift of the First Person of the Trinity, is not enough for salvation;
neither are the gifts of Christ. God therefore grants to man the gift of
grace, which transforms his nature and makes him capable of doing
good and being saved. A modern theologian defines grace as "the
Divinely infused supernatural quality which permanently divinizes the

4. This does not imply that the poem is a recounting of the spiritual education of the
Dreamer. There may be something of this, but it is incidental to the poet's main purpose: to inform his audience and move them to those actions necessary for their salvation. Robertson and Huppé tend to make the poem a kind of *Bildungsroman,* in which
a question by the Dreamer is an indication of spiritual blindness (e.g. pp. 210-11),
rather than a device by the poet to introduce a particular doctrine and to manage the
forward movement of the poem.

5. Though some points in the Catholic doctrine of grace were under debate in the
poet's day, the main points had been established. Cf. the *Summa Theologica,* I-II, qq.
109-14.

human nature to make it proportionate to its Divine end." [6] A four-teenth-century sermon explains it more simply as that by which "euery man and wymman may so gouerne hyme þat aftur is dethe he may com to þe blisse." [7]

The gift of the Holy Ghost confirms man's power to obey the law of love, as St. Augustine makes clear:

> And on the completion of fifty days from His resurrection He sent to them the Holy Spirit (for so He had promised), by whose agency they were to have love shed abroad in their hearts [Rom. v.5], to the end that they might be able to fulfill the law, not only without the sense of its being burdensome, but even with a joyful mind. This law was given to the Jews in the ten commandments, which they call the Decalogue. And these commandments, again, are reduced to two, namely, that we should love God with all our heart, with all our soul, with all our mind; and that we should love our neighbor as ourselves [Matt. xxii.37–40].[8]

Throughout *Dobest* charity is the poet's universal theme.

By the fourteenth century the Church had become the custodian of the gift of grace and had institutionalized it in the seven sacraments.[9] Grace was given to man through the sacrament of baptism, and increased by reception of the other sacraments.[1] Grace and its accompanying virtues were destroyed by mortal sin and could be restored only by the sacrament of penance. In *Dobest* only two sacraments are stressed, the eucharist and penance. They, unlike the others, could be received as often as desired, and by all Christians. It was principally through them that grace was transmitted to man in his daily struggle for salvation, and they are the sacraments which moralists and preachers exhorted their fellow men to take. The eucharist is the principal means by which grace is increased.[2] But before taking the eucharist one must be in a state of grace. Otherwise the act of taking the eucharist only

6. E. L. van Becelaere, "Grace, Doctrine of (Roman Catholic)," *Encyclopaedia of Religion and Ethics* (New York, Charles Scribner's Sons; and Edinburgh, T. and T. Clark, 1908–27), 6, 368. Cf. *Summa Theologica*, III, q. 62, i.

7. *Sermons*, p. 26.

8. *On the Catechizing of the Uninstructed*, trans. S. D. F. Salmond, NP-N, 3, 308 (chap. 23).

9. For a history of the Church's attitude toward the Sacraments, see Elizabeth Frances Rogers, *Peter Lombard and the Sacramental System* (New York, 1917), pp. 1–77.

1. *Summa Theologica*, III, q. 65, iii. The principal effect of the sacraments, St. Thomas says, is to increase grace: III, q. 62, esp. i, iii, and iv. A fourteenth-century preacher said God established the seven sacraments, "þe wiche shall esely brynge vs to þe blisse ʒiff we be of goode gouernaunce." *Sermons*, p. 30. For a popular treatise on the sacraments, see *Handlyng Synne*, Pt. II, ed. F. J. Furnivall, EETS, o.s. *123* (London, 1903), 297–349 (lines 9493–11,302).

2. *Summa Theologica*, III, q. 65, iii.

adds sin to the soul. Therefore if one has sinned he must first be restored to grace through the sacrament of penance.

Penance had a long history of controversy. The Church's power to
forgive sin was based particularly on Matthew xvi: 19,[3] in which the
power of the keys was granted by Christ to Peter. After a long struggle,
doctrinal and jurisdictional,[4] the Church had established penance as a
sacrament, taught that it removed mortal sin and restored men to
grace, instituted the practice of private confession, and granted the
power of the keys (i.e. the right to hear confession, impose penance,
and pronounce absolution) to priests as well as bishops. The poet apparently accepted these tenets, though he stresses some aspects of
penance and neglects others.

A development in the previous century had enormously increased the
importance of penance in the scheme of salvation. The Fourth Lateran
Council (1215) in its twenty-first canon, *Omnis utriusque sexus,* or-
dered all the faithful, after they had reached years of discretion, to confess their sins privately to their own priest at least once a year, and
to take communion at least at Easter. Otherwise entrance to the Church
was to be denied to the living, and Christian burial to the dead.[5] A modern historian says of this action, "The salutary discipline of penance
was converted into a compulsory test of fitness for a share in the full
privileges of membership of the Church, without which man was de-
barred from the hope of eternal salvation." [6] It is not difficult to see
how the fourteenth-century poet of *Piers Plowman* might come to re-
gard penance as the key sacrament for salvation, for it had become "a
compulsory test of fitness," and by it the gift of grace was made prac-
ticably available to the sinful wayfarer.

One must remember, finally, in reading *Dobest,* that there were difficulties and differences of opinion in the fourteenth century about the
relative importance of the three steps in penance, contrition of heart,

---

3. "Et tibi (Petro) dabo claues regni caelorum. Et quodcumque ligaueris super terram, erit ligatum & in caelis: & quodcumque solueris super terram, erit solutum & in
caelis." Cf. also Matthew xviii: 18 and John xx: 22–3.

4. For a history of the controversies over the doctrine of penance see Henry Charles
Lea, *A History of Auricular Confession and Indulgences in the Latin Church* (Philadel-
phia, 1896), *1* and *2,* esp. *1.* Also John T. McNeill, "Penance in the Ancient Church," in
the introduction to *Medieval Handbooks of Penance,* ed. John T. McNeill and Helena M.
Gamer, Columbia Records of Civilization, *29* (New York, 1938), 3–22; E. Mangenot,
"Confession dans la Bible," *DTC, 3,* Pt. I, 828–38; E. Vacandard, "Confession du Ier
au XIIIe siècle," ibid., 838–94; P. Bernard, "Confession (Du Concile de Latran au
Concile de Trente)," ibid., 894–926.

5. For a translation of this canon see *Handbooks of Penance,* pp. 413–14. For the
Latin text, see *Corpus Iuris Canonici* (Decretals of Pope Gregory IX), Bk. V, title
xxxviii, "De Poenitentiis et Remissionibus," chap. xii, p. 718.

6. Alexander Hamilton Thompson, "Medieval Doctrine to the Lateran Council of
1215," *Cambridge Medieval History* (Cambridge, England, Cambridge University
Press, 1911–36), *6,* 691.

confession of mouth, and satisfaction of works (the working out of the penance imposed by the priest). Which of the three actions did in fact secure forgiveness for the sinner? If contrition, then confession, and the role of the Church, became subordinate. If confession, or confession and satisfaction, then contrition seemed unnecessary, and penance became a mechanical process. The one position conflicted with the authority of the Church, jealous of its custodianship of the sacraments. The other conflicted with the authority of the Old and New Testaments and the writings of the Church Fathers.[7] As a compromise, it was generally agreed that contrition was essential, but true contrition had to include a desire to confess and was complete only when that vow was fulfilled, unless circumstances made confession impossible.[8] Nevertheless, there continued to be disagreements. Heretics in the thirteenth and fourteenth centuries stressed contrition and minimized the confessional act.[9] The friars were accused of minimizing contrition and stressing confession, a fact of considerable importance in the narrative of *Dobest*. The poet believed in all three stages of penance, but he was especially interested in contrition, as *Dobest* shows.

These beliefs about contrition, penance, the eucharist, and grace run through *Dobest*. Their interrelationship is most important. Contrition is necessary for penance; penance is necessary if one is to take the eucharist and be in a state of grace; grace, the gift of the Holy Ghost, is essential for salvation. This relationship would be familiar enough to a fourteenth-century audience, and the narrative and discussion in *Dobest* further establish these interconnections. Contrition, penance, and the eucharist, therefore, are related to the gift of the Holy Ghost, grace, and are thereby related to man's salvation.

These beliefs, however, do not participate as actively in the narrative of *Dobest* as one might expect. This is probably the main reason why *Dobest* is so difficult to analyze. The faculties of the soul appear as characters in *Dowel;* Christ is a protagonist in *Dobet*. *Dobest,* however, frequently presents a human scene with human actors. This is the poet's solution of a very difficult artistic problem, the problem of treating the gift of grace dramatically. His material in *Dowel,* the intellectual soul, gave him an aggregate of faculties and processes from which to choose his characters. His theme in *Dobet* gave him characters and narrative ready-made, for he had the Christ story as his material, though he went beyond this at some points. But the material

7. Numerous references to contrition in the Bible, the Fathers, and the scholastics are collected in P. Bernard's article "Contrition. Aspect Dogmatique," *DTC, 3,* Pt. II, 1671–86. For a medieval collection of references see Petrus Cantor, *Verbum Abbreviatum,* PL, *205,* cols. 340–2, 346–9. One text which the poet quotes is Psalm li: 17 (Vulgate 19).

8. Lea, *Auricular Confession, 1,* 142–55.

9. Bernard, "Contrition," col. 1674.

in *Dobest* did not allow such direct treatment. The Holy Ghost and grace are as abstract and doctrinally difficult as anything in Christian theology. And grace is a state, not a faculty or process, and so is almost impossible to dramatize. All that the gift of grace offers as narrative is the granting of the gift at Pentecost. The poet utilized this, but it was not much. He was a moralist and an artist, however, not a professor of systematic theology. Throughout *Dowel, Dobet, and Dobest* his concern is not with the scheme of salvation as such but with its significance for mankind. It is not the scheme which interests him but the salvation of man which it makes possible. In *Dobest,* therefore, it is not the Holy Ghost and the doctrine of grace itself which is the primary object of his attention but grace in its relation to man and his salvation. The human scene of so much of *Dobest* is the poet's solution of his artistic problem, the treatment of the highly abstract doctrine of grace. At the same time his concern for the human condition in *Dobest,* while more explicit than in *Dowel* and *Dobet,* in no sense represents a shift in emphasis.

The interlude which precedes the first vision of *Dobest* shows the Dreamer going to Church on Easter morn, "To here holy the masse · and to be houseled after." [1] The brief scene turns the reader's attention toward the Church and focuses not on its administrative but on its sacramental function. It reminds the reader that the Church is the custodian of the gift of grace for mankind. The reference to the eucharist is also a preparation for a development in the narrative of the first vision, the impasse at its conclusion over the proper condition to be met before taking the eucharist.

The first scene in the vision proper is a glimpse of Piers Plowman, "paynted al blody,' but in the likeness of Jesus. This leads to a long sermon by Conscience on the theme of Christ the conqueror, the freer of mankind.[2] Discussion of Christ even though *Dobet* has concluded can be justified because the life of Christ on earth did not end with the Resurrection, the culmination of *Dobet.* But this cannot explain all of Conscience's sermon, since it reviews the life of Christ from the beginning. Like the speech of Soul at the beginning of *Dobet,* it is an extended transition. The poet likes to carry the subject matter of one section into a new section before unfolding new material to his audience.

---

1. XIX.1–5. Skeat notes that it was an Easter mass: *Parallel Texts, 2, 265.* Penance was particularly associated with Lent, especially since the Easter mass had, in effect, been made compulsory by the decree of the Fourth Lateran Council, described above. For references in *Piers Plowman* associating penance with Lent, see esp. XII.175–82 (C.xv.114–21); also xx.355–9 (C.xxiii.357–61). Cf. also *Lay Folks Catechism,* ed. Thomas Frederick Simmons and Henry Edward Nolloth, EETS, o.s. *118* (London, 1901), 66, 67 (T version, lines 316–27; L version, lines 1029–40); John Myrc, *Instructions for Parish Priests,* ed. E. Peacock, EETS, o.s. *31* (London, 1868), 8 (lines 234–43); *Handlyng Synne,* p. 317 (lines 10,167 ff.).

2. XIX.5–193.

Conscience's long sermon serves that purpose, maintains historical continuity, and provides the first glimpse of the new doctrines offered in *Dobest.* Christ comes now with His cross, Conscience tells the Dreamer,

> . . . to wissen vs there-wyth · that whan that we ben tempted,
> Ther-with to fyȝte and fenden vs · fro fallyng in-to synne,
> And se bi his sorwe · that who so loueth Ioye,
> To penaunce and to pouerte · he moste putten hym-seluen,
> And moche wo in this worlde · willen and suffren.[3]

At the conclusion of his sermon Conscience introduces the theme proper of the first vision of *Dobest:* Christ gave Piers (mankind, as well as the Apostle Peter) power to forgive men their sins if they will pay as their pardon *redde quod debes.*

An explication of *redde quod debes* will be more appropriate at the conclusion of the first vision, where it precipitates a crisis in the narrative. Conscience himself, however, deserves a word of comment. He is the first character to appear in *Dobest,* and he is the most important character in these last two visions. Grace or the Holy Paraclete will tell mankind to make Conscience their king,[4] and the poet himself calls Conscience keeper and guide of Christians.[5] Conscience, who taught Haukyn the three steps of penance, is the human faculty which enables man to retain, or more important, to regain grace. He enables man to avoid evil, and to repent truly when he has sinned.

When the sermon has ended,[6] announcing Piers' pardon in return

---

3. xix.60–4.
4. xix.251.
5. xx.71–2.
6. One problem in the sermon of Conscience is the meaning of the passage in which Conscience applies the terms Dowel, Dobet, and Dobest to Christ's life: xix.104–93; specific reference to the terms occurs at 106, 112, 119 (Dowel), 125 (Dobet), 177 (Dobest). Conscience says Christ began Dowel when He taught man to love his enemies; Dobet when He performed miracles; and Dobest when He granted man the power of forgiveness of sins. This is the only use of the terms in the text after *Dowel.* Coghill believes the terms here as elsewhere mean the Three Lives and that the poet is saying Christ lived them Himself: introduction to Wells' trans. of *Piers Plowman,* p. xxiii, and *MedAev, 2,* 123. But the details of the passage do not fit the pattern of the Three Lives. As I have noted (above, p. 80, n. 1), the performance of miracles, which is called Dobet here, is the active, not the contemplative, aspect of Christ's life. The passage on Dobest in Christ's life stresses not so much the Church's role in the forgiveness of sins, which might be interpreted as the Mixed Life, but rather the layman's role: he must pay *redde quod debes.* Mensendieck suggested that the terms in Conscience's sermon were a kind of guide to the *Dowel, Dobet,* and *Dobest* sections (*Charakterentwickelung,* pp. 60–1). The suggestion is plausible. Dowel in Christ's life corresponds to part of the theme of *Dowel:* knowledge of the law of love. Dobest in the sermon corresponds to the theme of *Dobest,* man's power to secure forgiveness of sins, though the teaching of *redde quod debes* really applies only to the first vision of *Dobest.* But the passage on Dobet stresses Christ's miracles, which *Dobet* does not, and the passage does not refer to the freeing of man from the devil's power, which *Dobet* stresses. If the miracles and other incidents in the Dobet portion of Christ's life are examples of Christ's love which encourage man to obey the law of love, perhaps we

for *redde quod debes,* the Dreamer witnesses the coming of the Holy Paraclete and the granting of grace to mankind. Grace is a weapon to fight against sin, but specifically the passage shows mankind being assigned various gifts of labor. Grace is in fact shown as the wellspring of all human crafts. As a further aid to man, Grace grants other gifts— the four evangelists (that is, their writings), the four great Church Fathers, the four cardinal virtues, and Unity—that is, Holy Church— together with priesthood and the sacrament of penance (Contrition and Confession). All this is entrusted to Piers (mankind in its semi-divine aspect) and, to a lesser degree, to Conscience.[7] A period of history is shown here in a lightning flash—the early Christian era in which the Church was established, the Church being the custodian of the gift of grace.

A remarkable feature of this scene is the poet's transformation into gifts of labor of the gifts of grace described in Corinthians I, part of which is quoted. Phrases like "divisiones operationum sunt," and "Unicuique autem datur manifestatio Spiritus ad utilitatem" [8] may have suggested this interpretation to the poet. But the paraphrase of the passage goes beyond Paul's text. It reveals a fundamental tenet in the poet's thought, his belief that labor is God-given. The divinity of labor, the concept which creates the figure of Piers, is here expressed in the identification of the divisions of grace and the divisions of labor. The curse of Adam has become a blessing. Labor is a help against sin. Grace bids men crown Conscience king and make Craft (trade, the divisions of labor) their steward. Moreover, since the various crafts and estates are God-given, the divisions of labor should lead not to strife but to mutual love among men.[9] The passage in Paul on the divisions of grace is a plea against jealousy and animosity and for mutual love. It contains the famous image of the body and its members, an argument for harmony and mutual respect. Politically, the poet's plea is a plea against change, particularly against unrest among laborers. But he urges most strongly that the higher levels of society

---

can say the passage reveals part of the theme of *Dobet.* More probably, however, the poet, here as elsewhere, is using the terms as a device, this time to elaborate on the life of Christ. The passage is probably not related to *Dowel, Dobet, and Dobest* but to this first vision of *Dobest,* whose theme is the necessity of forgiving others if one would be forgiven his sins (*redde quod debes*)—in other words, the necessity of brotherly love. Christ taught this in Dobest, Conscience says, having already emphasized the doctrine of love by preaching that in Dowel Christ gave man the law of love and in Dobet He gave examples of love.

7. XIX.194–330.
8. I Corinthians xii : 1 ff.
9. The doctrine of love was frequently advanced as a remedy for the strife between the "estates" of medieval society: Ruth Mohl, *The Three Estates in Medieval and Renaissance Literature* (New York, 1933), pp. 369–76. Miss Mohl does not cite the striking application of this doctrine in *Piers Plowman.*

should not humiliate the lower, and behind the passage lies his vision of an era of universal peace and love. The scene preaches the law of love; for the estates of society, since they are divinely appointed, are obliged to obey the command to love one another.

In the second part of the scene with Grace the establishment of the Church is represented in an extended metaphor of plowing, sowing, and harvesting.[1] That Piers the Plowman may till Truth, Grace gives him the evangelists as his oxen, Unitas (Holy Church) as the barn for the harvested crop,[2] etc. The cardinal virtues are represented as essential for man's salvation, for each one is defined and discussed at some length, and in the metaphor of plowing and sowing they are the seeds which Piers is given by Grace (the Holy Spirit) to sow in man's heart. The cardinal virtues were gifts of the Holy Ghost, but so also were the three theological virtues and the seven gifts of the Holy Ghost. Why are the cardinal virtues so important here and elsewhere in the vision? The answer is that, according to the poet, the cardinal virtues endowed man with the power to love:

> Thise foure sedes Pieres sewe · and sitthe he did hem harwe
> Wyth olde lawe and newe lawe · that loue myȝte wexe
> Amonge the foure vertues · and vices destroye.[3]

A passage inserted in the B-text Prologue illuminates not only his conception of the virtues but the whole first vision of *Dobest:*

> I parceyued of the power · that Peter had to kepe,
> To bynde and to vnbynde · as the boke telleth,
> How he it left with loue · as owre lorde hight,
> Amonges foure vertues · the best of alle vertues,
> That cardinales ben called · and closyng ȝatis,
> There crist is in kyngdome · to close and to shutte,
> And to opne it to hem · and heuene blisse shewe.[4]

In the poet's mind the power to bind and unbind (the power of the keys), love, and the cardinal virtues seem to have been intertwined.

1. The metaphor may have been suggested by the parable of the sowing of the seed in Matthew xiii.

2. The details of the barn are clear enough. Grace gives Piers the materials. The timbers are the cross and the crown of thorns; the mortar is called mercy, made of Christ's baptism and blood; Grace wattles and walls the barn with Christ's pains and Passion. Holy Writ is the roof. In other words, the Church is ordained by Christ—by His sacrifice on the cross. Robertson and Huppé, *Scriptural Tradition*, p. 222, n. 11, refer to St. Augustine, Sermon LXXIII, PL, *38*, col. 471, for the significance of the barn. Cf. this passage from the *Miroure of Mans Saluacionne*, p. 114, on Christ's building the Church: "ffor crist . . . has made on kyrke be his mercy And in this werke in stede of Cyment oure lord Jhū toke his haly blode And his precyous body for stones for oure luf hanged on the rode."

3. XIX.306–8.

4. Pr. 100–6.

To be forgiven one's sins one must love, and the cardinal virtues help man to obey the law of love.

It is difficult to say to what extent this treatment of the cardinal virtues is peculiar to the poet. Other medieval writers agree on the importance of the cardinal virtues, and some statements seem to equate them with the power of love. In Lyndwood's *Provinciale* a canon quoted from Peccham says of the cardinal virtues, "per quas ad seipsum & proximum homo ordinatur." And Lyndwood glosses *cardinales* by saying, "Sic dictae, quia sicut ostium vertitur in cardine, ita in his vertitur & regitur vita hominis." [5] Petrus Cantor said that by them was shown the perfection of the Christian life.[6] Gregory said that good works are based on these virtues, and that in them the mind is carried to the topmost height of perfection. He even seems to subordinate the seven gifts of the Holy Ghost to them: "For the gift of the Spirit, which, in the mind It works on, forms first of all Prudence, Temperance, Fortitude, Justice, in order that the same mind may be perfectly fashioned to resist every species of assault, doth afterwards give it a temper in the seven virtues." [7] And St. Augustine is closer yet to the poet's conception of the cardinal virtues when he speaks of virtue as nothing else than perfect love of God, and the fourfold division of virtue as four forms of love.[8]

Most of these ideas are combined in the popular treatise *The Book of Vices and Virtues*. The ancient philosophers speak much of these four virtues, says the book, "but þe Holy Gost ȝeueþ hem moche bettre and techeþ hem an hundred so wel." [9] Augustine's statement about the virtues is repeated, and the discussion closes with a burst of praise:

> And wiþ-oute þes foure vertues þar may no man clymbe vp to þe hille of parfiȝtnesse. For who-so wole clymbe so hiȝe, hym bihoueþ first þat he haue prudence, þat mowe make hym first despise þe world; and strengþe þerwiþ, þat mowe ȝeue good herte and myȝty to vndertake grete þinges and to folewe þer-on; and on þat oþere syde þat he haue attemperaunce, so þat he ne be not to moche charged; and justice þer-wiþ, þat mowe lede hym þe riȝt weyes and þat mowe schewe hym þe kyngdom of God. . . . Who-so hadde þes foure vertues, he schulde be wel parfiȝt and blessed in þis world and more in þat oþer, for he schulde be in pees of herte & spirituel ioye; noþing scholde faile hym, but euere he scholde wexe

5. *Provinciale*, pp. 62–3.
6. *Verbum Abbreviatum*, chap. cxv, PL, *205*, col. 305. He discusses each virtue in a separate chapter, chaps. cxvi–cxix, cols. 305–9.
7. *Morals on the Book of Job*, Oxford translation (Oxford, 1844), *1*, 119. For Gregory's discussion of the cardinal virtues see pp. 118–19.
8. *On the Morals of the Catholic Church*, trans. Richard Stothert, NP-N, 1, *4*, 48 (chap. 15). See also 51–5 (chaps. 19–25).
9. P. 122.

more and more in God, þat he schulde alwey bere wiþ-ynne hym, in whom he schulde haue his likynge and his delit.[1]

The doctrine, both here and in the poem, seems to be that the cardinal virtues, gifts of the Holy Ghost, help man to avoid sin and do good works, preserve grace, and lead the good life which secures salvation, the essence of the virtuous life being, of course, to love God and one's neighbor.[2]

The gifts of the Holy Ghost have been distributed. Henceforth, to the conclusion of *Dobest,* the poem will examine man's use of these gifts. Sin still exists. There is still the world, the flesh, and the devil. But sin can be resisted. Man will not be sinless, even though the state of grace helps him to fight sin. But by virtue of the gifts of the Holy Ghost he can repent and refuse sin, be contrite, do penance, and be restored to grace.

This is not an issue for the poet to treat historically. It is the salvation of his own generation which agitates him. He shifts the scene to his own day and shows mankind attacked by Pride, the deadliest of the deadly sins, and by the Lord of Lust. Pride is powerful, and man cannot go against him unless grace is with him. But under the guidance of Conscience and Kynde Wit men do deeds of penance and are truly contrite. As a consequence, Unitas stands in holiness, and Conscience invites the company of the faithful to receive the eucharist. Man can fight sin and be in a state of grace if he is truly penitent.[3] It is a triumphant moment in the drama.

The triumph, alas, is short-lived. Conscience's invitation to receive the eucharist is conditional on man's having paid *redde quod debes* for the pardon of Piers Plowman (i.e. forgiveness of sins).[4] And the people balk at this condition. The ill-tempered, brawling argument which follows, involving a cross-section of society, reveals that mankind has abandoned the cardinal virtues, and it is clear there is little love between men.[5] The brewer cheats. The cardinals are a burden and a menace by their extravagance and lechery. The pope commands Christians to kill one another.[6] The commune transmutes the cardinal virtue

---

1. P. 125. In the *Miroure of Mans Saluacionne,* p. 42, the cardinal virtues are called "The rotes of alle vertues forto destruye alle vice."
2. Burdach has an interesting discussion of the treatment of the cardinal virtues in Aquinas, Dante, and Langland: *Ackermann,* pp. 302–3.
3. XIX.331–88.
4. XIX.389–93.
5. XIX.394–473.
6. Quite possibly the poet here is attacking the Anti-Pope, Clement VII, who was especially hated by the English because they considered him a tool of the French. See Bernard F. Huppé, "The Date of the B-text of *Piers Plowman," SP, 38* (1941), 41–4. Huppé explains the attack on the cardinals at XIX.413–21 as an attack on the French cardinals who elected Clement. See also Bennett, *MedAev, 12,* 62–3. Bennett suggests the poet is criticizing Urban rather than Clement.

of prudence into guile. For the lord of the manor intellect [7] and fortitude become a cunning and merciless extortion of feudal dues. And a
king argues that because he is the law, he can take anything with
perfect justice. The happy society projected in the divisions of labor
is not here. As Conscience warns the king that he must be bound by
reason, truth, and law, the Dreamer wakes.[8]

The vision ends indecisively. Dramatically, there is an unexpected
reversal. The eucharist is not received. Mankind, or a portion of it, is
not in a state of grace. Absolution cannot be pronounced, because the
people have refused to pay *redde quod debes.*

What is *redde quod debes?* The poet's explanation of the phrase and
the narrative context provide the first clue. When Conscience tells mankind it must pay *redde quod debes* before receiving the eucharist, there
is the following interchange:

> "How?" quod al the comune · "thow conseillest vs to ȝelde
>   Al that we owen any wyȝte · ar we go to housel?"
> "That is my conseille," quod Conscience · "and cardynale vertues,
>   That vche man forȝyue other · and that wyl the *paternoster,*
>   *Et dimitte nobis debita nostra, etc.,*
>   And so to ben assoilled · and sithen ben houseled." [9]

Skeat thought the phrase meant the sinner was not pardoned until he
tried to make restitution.[1] The phrase meant that in part, for in penance
the sinner was obliged, if he could, to make restitution of goods stolen
or obtained through trickery, before receiving absolution. The *Pupilla
oculi,* a manual for priests, in the section "De forma restitutionis et
quando res est restituenda et quando non," states: "Non dimittitur
peccatum nisi restituatur ablatum si restitui potest. . . . Oportet ergo
ut de omnibus dampnis et de rebus iniuriose acquisitis fiat restitutio.
Vel ad minus habeat firmum propositum restituendi si quid ab alio
iniuriose ablatum est antequam valeat satisfactio sacramentalis. Non
tamen est restitutio pars satisfactionis huius sed ad eam quoddam pre-
ambulum." [2] The characters who resist Conscience's command of *redde*

7. Not properly one of the cardinal virtues but one of the gifts of the Holy Ghost.
8. xix.474–8.
9. xix.389–93.
1. *Parallel Texts, 2,* 268. Skeat cites in support of this C.vii.316, 322 (B.v. 469, 475).
2. Johannis de Burgo, *Pupilla oculi* . . . (Paris, 1510), xxxiʳ. The opening clause,
"Non dimittitur peccatum nisi restituatur ablatum," is almost identical with the Latin
quoted at C.vii.257: "Nunquam dimittitur peccatum, nisi restituatur ablatum." Skeat,
Parallel Texts, 2, 87, quoted St. Augustine, Epistle cliii, sec. 20; *Opera,* ed. Migne, *2,*
662: "non remittetur peccatum, nisi resᵗituatur ablatum." St. Augustine is probably
the ultimate source of the line, but it had become common property, as is indicated by
its appearance in the *Pupilla oculi* and in the Canon of Walter, "Sacerdos in poenitentia
injungenda." See Lyndwood, *Provinciale,* Bk. V, title 16, chap. vii, pp. 332–3. Though
the *Pupilla oculi* expressly states that restitution is not part of the sinner's satisfaction
but a kind of preamble to it, restitution, or rather that larger doctrine of *redde quod
debes* which probably included restitution, may have been more or less identified in the

quod debes are patently a group of greedy swindlers fighting the suggestion that they return ill-gotten gains. *Radix omnium malorum est cupiditas.* The Lady Meed episode preached that lesson. Cupidity is the enemy of love, which is the essence of human virtue. On this the poet and the Church are agreed. Cupidity in this scene has killed the cardinal virtues, i.e. love, in the hearts of men.

It is to this larger issue of love that the scene moves. The words of Conscience show that the phrase *redde quod debes* meant more than the restitution of stolen goods.[3] Man must forgive others their sins to him before being pardoned. Needless to say, the forgiveness of others is a basic Christian doctrine. It is enjoined in the Pater Noster and elsewhere in the New Testament,[4] and it is illustrated in the parable from which the phrase *redde quod debes* comes. The parable is the story of

---

poet's mind with satisfaction. Certain remarks in the *Pupilla oculi* suggest how this identification might occur: "secundum Anselmum, ii. cur deus homo. Satisfacere: est deo honorem debitum reddere. Satisfactio enim curat peccata preterita recompensando" (xxxᵛ). The phrase from Anselm brings us closer to the poet's phrase, "redde quod debes," and links also with the important passage from Romans quoted below, "Reddite ergo omnibus debita . . . cui honorem, honorem." "Restitution" may have been a current controversial issue, particularly in the attacks made by the "possessioners" on the friars. In 1354 Archbishop Fitzralph attacked the friars for their failure to demand satisfaction and restitution as a condition for absolution: " 'vnde dampnant se confessores religiosi si qui sunt et alij qui receptis paucis denariis non inducta restitucione hominem de furto aut de vsura aut de iniusto lucro proximi absolucionem impendunt.' " Cited by Aubrey Gwynn, "Archbishop FitzRalph," *Studies, 25* (1936), 83. A similar complaint appears in a bill delivered to the Convocation of Canterbury in May 1356. It charges, among other things, that the friars "abuse their powers as confessors and dispense freely from the duty of restitution." From the summary by Aubrey Gwynn, "Archbishop FitzRalph and the Friars," *Studies, 26* (1937), 51. The Latin text of the complaint is given in W. A. Pantin, *The English Church in the Fourteenth Century* (Cambridge, England, Cambridge University Press, 1955), pp. 267–8, together with a translation, pp. 159–60. According to Pantin's translation, however, the charge is that the friars "convert to their own gain" the compensation that should be restored to the injured party. But the Latin seems uncertain. A manual for parish priests written for an English audience by a Doctor of Canon Law at Avignon in 1344, the "Memoriale Presbiterorum" (or "Memoriale Sacerdotum") devotes one of its three parts to the problem of restitution. The manual has a "marked anti-mendicant bias" (Pantin, p. 206), and in one of the passages cited by Pantin (p. 209) accuses the mendicant orders of being especially lax in requiring restitution of plunderers in war. *Piers Plowman* does not bring the friars into the discussion of the necessity of restitution, and it puts the burden of responsibility and blame on those seeking absolution. But "restitution" may still have been an issue when the poem was written. The poet also insists on restitution at v.276 ff. and XVII.304.

3. On the importance of restitution see above and also *Lay Folks Catechism*, pp. 56, 57 (T version, lines 244–7; L version, lines 874–6); *Speculum Christiani*, p. 32; *Speculum Sacerdotale*, ed. Edward H. Weatherly, EETS, o.s. 200 (London, 1936), 71; Lea, *Auricular Confession, 2*, 43–7 ff.

4. The Pater Noster in Matthew is followed by these words: "Si enim dimiseritis hominibus peccata eorum: dimittet & vobis pater vester caelestis delicta vestra. Si autem non dimiseritis hominibus: nec pater vester dimittet vobis peccata vestra" (Matthew vi: 14–15). And cf. Mark xi: 25–6: "Et cum stabitis ad orandum, dimittite si quid habetis adversus aliquem: ut & Pater vester qui in caelis est, dimittat vobis peccata vestra. Quod si vos non dimiseritis: nec Pater vester, qui in caelis est, dimittet vobis peccata vestra."

the servant who, after being forgiven a large debt by his lord, turns on a fellow servant and demands payment of a lesser debt owed him— *redde quod debes*. When the fellow servant cannot pay, he casts him into prison. Hearing this, the lord hands over the unforgiving servant to the torturers.[5] The story preaches the same doctrine as the command from the Pater Noster, that God will not forgive man's sins unless he first forgives those who have sinned against him.[6] This association of the forgiveness of others with penance was not original with the poet. Long before penance had become an established sacrament, forgiving others the injuries they had done the penitent was one of the (usually seven) traditional ways to secure remission of sins.[7] When penance became a formal sacrament, "the forgiveness of injuries and the eradication from the heart of all sentiments of hatred" remained a "requisite essential to the validity of confession." [8] It was part of the process of confession for the confessor to ask the penitent if he forgave his enemies.[9]

The poet did not make a stumbling block out of the forgiveness of others simply because it was part of the process of penance. He was not interested in technicalities. He was interested only in the largest issues. To think of *redde quod debes* as nothing more than part of the sacrament of penance is to miss the poet's purpose in choosing the phrase. It is its larger significance that concerns him. The command to forgive others is, like the similar command to love one's enemies, essentially the precept love thy neighbor. The debt referred to in *redde*

5. Matthew xviii: 21–35. The parable is told in answer to Peter's question, "Lord, how oft shall my brother sin against me, and I forgive him? till seven times?"

6. See the commentaries of the Fathers, especially that of Augustine, in *Catena Aurea*, II, 646, 647. A sermon preached on the text *redde quod debes* also interprets the parable as a command to forgive others: *Sermons*, pp. 36–45. Petrus Cantor refers to the parable when discussing forgiveness of others: *Verbum Abbreviatum*, chap. xcix, "De misericordia ignoscente," PL, *205*, col. 281.

7. Lea, *Auricular Confession*, *1*, 80–3; *Medieval Handbooks of Penance*, pp. 99 n., 100, 152, 396, 410–11; Alain de Lille, *Liber Poenitentialis*, PL, *210*, col. 298.

8. Lea, *Auricular Confession*, *2*, 41. For example, a statement in *Speculum Sacerdotale*, p. 71, reads: "tho men owen noȝt to be asoylid that wol noȝt come out of here hatredyn and wraþe, ne wol noȝt foryeve wrongis þat be done to hem, ne a-corden ȝif the partie come and profre satisfaccion or lowly wolde aske of hem foryeuenes and mercy."

9. See *Medieval Handbooks of Penance*, pp. 316, 324; cf. also Myrc, *Parish Priests*, lines 1453–4. It is also one of seven questions which "a Curat aught to aske euery cristene persone that liethe in the extremytie of dethe" (pp. 63 f.). Cf. also *English Fragments from Latin Medieval Service-Books*, ed. Henry Littlehales, EETS, e.s. 90 (London, 1903), 8, and *Pupilla oculi*, lxxi^r. Forgiveness of others, it should be noted, was sometimes classified as a form of alms: cf. *Speculum Christiani*, p. 4, and chap. 73 of St. Augustine's *Enchiridion*, NP-N, *3*, 261, entitled "The Greatest of all Alms is to Forgive our Debtors and to Love our Enemies." As alms it might be considered a form of satisfaction; so Chaucer's Parson treated it: *The Complete Works of Chaucer*, ed. Fred N. Robinson (Cambridge, Mass., Houghton Mifflin Co., 1933), p. 312.

quod debes is man's debt of love to God and to his neighbor. A passage in Romans xiii, which the poet apparently knew,[1] reveals this:

> Reddite ergo omnibus debita : cui tributum, tributum : cui vectigal, vectigal : cui timorem, timorem : cui honorem, honorem.
>   Nemini quidquam debeatis : nisi ut invicem diligatis : qui enim diligit proximum, legem implevit. Nam : Non adulterabis : Non occides : Non furaberis : Non falsum testimonium dices : Non concupisces : et si quod est aliud mandatum, in hoc verbo instauratur : Diliges proximum tuum sicut teipsum. Dilectio proximi malum non operatur. Plenitudo ergo legis est dilectio.

Love is the fulfillment of the law. The debt man must pay to secure forgiveness of sins and restoration to grace—*redde quod debes*—is love. "For he that is dettour to God ne yeldeth nat to God al his dette, that is to seyn, al the love of his herte." [2] Love of God and neighbor, expressed in the forgiveness of others, is an essential part of penance. Contrition and repentance are essential also. The second vision of *Dobest* preaches that lesson. But if a man is contrite and repents and yet does not forgive others, he cannot be forgiven himself. That is, he cannot be absolved and restored to grace. This is the lesson of the first vision. Man has not paid the debt of love on which his pardon depends. He has not fulfilled the law—the law of penance in the narrower sense of the phrase *redde quod debes,* and the law of Christ in the broader sense. Even the king must obey civil law, Conscience boldly declares as the vision ends. The warning is clear enough: How much more must man obey God's law, *redde quod debes,* the law of love, the restitution of goods and the forgiveness of others.

The second vision of *Dobest* employs much the same scene and narrative pattern as the latter part of the first vision. It is the real, contemporary world again, and the narrative is one of warfare and siege. Unitas is attacked by the sins, and Conscience is defeated in a last-minute reversal of fortune. But while scene and pattern are parallel in the two visions, detail and tone are not. The last vision intensifies both the scene and the action. The contemporary world is observed in close and realistic detail. The narrative is exciting and melodramatic, with hardly a moment of rest. There is almost no preaching of abstract doctrine, although the issue is still whether mankind will avail itself of the Holy Ghost's gift of grace, the cardinal virtues, and Unitas and

---

1. Apparently he quotes a word from the passage at v.469, 475: Skeat refers to Romans xiii : 7 in his note on the passage: *Notes to "Piers Plowman,"* EETS, o.s. 67 (London, 1877), 126. Henry Morley also thought the phrase *redde quod debes* was associated with Romans xiii : 7–8: *English Writers* (London, etc., 1889), 4, 349, n.
2. Chaucer, "The Parson's Tale," *Works,* p. 284.

so be saved. And the narrative, as always, is built on an idea and a message.

There is so much narrative that a brief summary will be useful for seeing the main outline of incident and the message it preaches. Preceding the vision is a long interlude in the real world in which the Dreamer, half-starved, meets Need, who praises a life of need.[3] Falling asleep, the Dreamer sees a world in chaos. Antichrist, aided by the mortal sins and evil friars and religious, is uprooting the crop of truth. This evil host attacks Conscience, who calls on Nature (Kynde) for help. Nature replies by sending the great plagues that ravaged England in the fourteenth century. This tremendous *memento mori,* however, fails to reform mankind.[4] Old Age at last persuades one man to remember his mortality and repent. It is the Dreamer himself. Nature tells him the old lesson: learn to love, and the needs of the body will be cared for (*ne solliciti sitis*). And so by contrition and confession (true penance) the Dreamer comes to Unity.[5]

Unity, however, with Conscience as constable, is being savagely besieged by Antichrist's army. Conscience cries to Clergy for help, but refuses aid from the friars, for Need says they are untrustworthy because of their poverty. Conscience urges them to reform, and to limit their numbers.[6] They ignore his counsel.[7] Conscience is helped most

3. xx.1–49.
4. xx.50–163.
5. xx.164–212.
6. The opponents of the friars complained of their rapid growth. Cf. "Fifty Heresies and Errors of Friars," *Select Wycliff, 3,* 400. More than mere jealousy was involved. Richard Fitzralph, Archbishop of Armagh, made much the same complaint as the poet (cf. xx.252–70). The limitless multiplication of friars, he said, was against both the law of nature, according to Aristotle, and the law of God. "But sich multiplicacioun y-founded vppon beggyng & beggerye, as freres telleþ, may nouȝt ordeyne a certeyn noumbre of persones þat þei schulde fynde, noþer þei mowe of certein oon person fynde" (*Defensio,* pp. 59–60). Cf. also the Wife of Bath's thrust at the number of the friars, *Canterbury Tales,* D, 864–77. Both Fitzralph and the poet attack the rapid growth of the friars in part as a consequence of their theoretical poverty. They are not limited, as the "possessioners" are, by the necessity of making a specific provision for the welfare of a new member. For the poet's attack on the theoretical poverty of the friars, see below. The attack on their unlimited membership here is one part of that attack, and one further piece of evidence linking the poet's attack with the discussion over the theoretical poverty of the friars in his day.
7. xx.213–94. Several interesting but minor points are made about the friars at xx.271–6. The statement that they go to school at Envy's bidding means they are motivated by envy—envy of the regular clergy and the monastic orders, presumably. The poet attacks their concentration on law and logic because he feels they study the law but do not obey its basic command, to love. Cf. Conscience's program for reform, xx.243–51. He also hates their logic-chopping and their sophistical treatment of penance. Cf. xix.341–7, where Pride's aides say the cardinal virtues and Unitas will be destroyed by covering contrition and confession with sophistry. The poet's attack on the friars' teaching of a kind of primitive communism has been misunderstood, I believe, by the critics, who see in it evidence only of the poet's orthodoxy in political economy: Skeat, *Parallel Texts, 2,* 283; Mensendieck, *Charakterentwickelung,* p. 73; Wells, "Notes," *The Vision of Piers Plowman,* p. 303. The passage on the friars'

by his surgeon, Contrition, but Contrition's medicine is too unpleasant, and Friar Flatterer gains a wheedling entry. The enemy is within the castle. Money payment to the friars replaces Contrition's salves, and when the sins attack once more,[8] Conscience calls in vain on Contrition to keep the gate:

> "He lith and dremeth," seyde Pees · "and so do many other;
> The frere with his phisik · this folke hath enchaunted
> And plastred hem so esyly · thei drede no synne."
> "Bi Cryste," quod Conscience tho · "I wil bicome a pilgryme,
> And walken as wyde · as al the worlde lasteth,
> To seke Piers the Plowman · that Pryde may destruye,
> And that freres hadde a fyndyng · that for nede flateren,
> And contrepleteth me, Conscience; · now Kynde me auenge,
> And sende me happe and hele · til I haue Piers the Plowman!"
> And sitthe he gradde after grace · til I gan awake.[9]

And with these words the vision, and *Dobest,* and the entire poem come to a close.

This final dream is clearly a vision of a wicked generation, warned of its wickedness by plagues sent from heaven, yet largely unheeding and unrepentant. The poet's purpose is to shake his fellow man out of his apathy and show him the dangers that threaten before it is too late. It is a cry for repentance and reform. The poet calls on mankind to see the evil in their own hearts. And at the same time he savagely exposes a danger to mankind from without. A main reason for the world's wickedness is evil men in the church. And of all evil churchmen, the friars are the greatest threat to man's salvation. The final scene of the vision is an overwhelming denunciation of the friars.

The indictment of evil churchmen which runs through the last vision receives symbolic expression in the figure of Antichrist. It would be easy to give Antichrist here a significance which the figure does not

---

communistic teaching is brief and leads directly into the attack on their invasion of the parish priest's jurisdiction in confession: xx.276–84. The point of the passage is this: the friars teach that all things ought to be in common, and therefore the priest's cure of souls is theirs too, and they have as much right to hear the parishioners' confessions as the priest.

8. xx.295–372. It is Contrition who asks that Friar Flatterer be allowed entrance. This seems inappropriate, but only if we assume that Contrition always stands for sincere contrition. Most of the sinners have already been wounded by Hypocrisy (xx.298, 301, 315), and it is explicitly stated that Contrition has been hurt by Hypocrisy (xx.331–3). In this scene, then, Contrition is insincere, hypocritical contrition, and his call for an easy confessor is understandable. Less understandable is Conscience's action in permitting them to call the Friar. He argue against the request, as he should, and then abruptly consents. Is conscience fallible too? Or are the demands of the narrative here stronger than the logic of the personification?

9. xx.375–84.

really possess. True, there are apocalyptic overtones to this vision, but in spite of its disasters, warnings, and brave hopes it is not a vision of the Last Judgment. Although doctrinally the appearance of Antichrist was a sign of approaching Doomsday, by the fourteenth century "Antichrist" had become a mere term of abuse.[1] That is how the poet uses Antichrist here. He says nothing about Doomsday. Antichrist suggests an enemy within the Church, and the poet's Antichrist heads an army composed of the sins allied with evil churchmen, religious, and the friars. The presence of these evil ecclesiastics in Antichrist's army is stressed again and again.[2] Their presence distinguishes this army from the army of sins in the preceding vision. The result, of course, is the evil triumph of the friars. Antichrist, therefore, means either the pope,[3] as the one responsible for this league of ecclesiastics and sin, or else all Christians, but especially churchmen, who by their evil lives or corruptions of doctrines and sacraments lead men to sin rather than to grace. Antichrist is the human ally of sin, not the precursor of Judgment Day. His appearance is an indictment and a warning against present evils, not a sign of the Second Coming.

There are attacks on evil churchmen throughout the last vision, but the fiercest charge is against the friars. The narrative ultimately focuses on them. They cause the final catastrophe. They are the villains. To understand the primary message of the last vision one must understand exactly what is meant by the talk about the friars. It cannot be dismissed as obsessive hatred for the fraternal orders. It is built integrally into the narrative structure.

The attack on the friars really begins in the interlude preceding the vision. The interlude is a preparation for the poet's analysis of the root cause of the friars' corruption of Christendom. The final betrayal of Unitas by Friar Flatterer is the result of his easy confessions. He grants, for "a pryue payement," for "a litel siluer," absolution without contrition. Man is no longer contrite; he forgets "to crye and to wepe, And wake for his wykked werkes · as he was wont to done." He has abandoned contrition, "the souereynest salue for alkyn synnes."[4] But penance without contrition is not valid, and so man remains in a state of mortal sin instead of being restored to a state of grace. As a conse-

---

1. W. Bousset, "Antichrist," *Encyclopaedia of Religion and Ethics, 1,* 581. Cf. the use made of the term "Antichrist" in "The Plowman's Tale," lines 189–96, 493–500, 541–56, 813–20, 845–52, 917–24, 949–56; and in "Jack Upland," p. 191: *Chaucerian and Other Pieces, A Supplement to the Complete Works of Geoffrey Chaucer,* ed. W. W. Skeat, Oxford, 1897.

2. xx.57–68; 125–7; 214–28.

3. Mensendieck, *Charakterentwickelung,* pp. 68–71, suggests, though very tentatively, that Antichrist is the pope. He remarks that the poet is not very clear on this point. He cites C.xxiii.126 ff. B.xx.125 ff. omits the reference to the pope, but Donaldson, p. 242, believes the C-text reading is correct for B also.

4. xx.362–70.

quence, the Holy Ghost's gifts of grace, Unitas, the cardinal virtues, and penance all come to nought. Friars do this work of evil. Why do they thus contradict the dictates of conscience, which incites men to contrition? Because of their need. This is the charge made by Conscience which concludes the poem: "freres . . . for nede flateren And contrepleteth me, Conscience. . . ." Need is the cause of their fatal activities. No statement could be clearer. And Need is the speaker and the subject in the overture to this vision.

The purpose of Need's speech [5] is to expose the philosophy of need which motivates the friars. Though need is praised in the speech, the praise is ironic. Conscience's remark about need in the conclusion would be proof enough, but there is also evidence in the speech itself that this persuasive sermon is not to be taken at face value. Need unblushingly urges doctrines which the poet has vigorously opposed elsewhere in the poem. Need is within the limits of orthodoxy in saying men have the right to take without payment food, drink, and clothing to preserve life.[6] But he debases his argument when he appeals for precedent to the lawless king and the corrupt commune in the preceding vision, who used need as an excuse for cupidity and the neglect of the cardinal virtues. Need also preaches a doctrine of morality unacceptable within the context of the poem. He is right, after a fashion, when he observes that men often err in practicing the cardinal virtues; but he is wrong when he argues from this that temperance is the only virtue and that need is next to God, Who governs all virtues. This argument makes need the sole principle of morality. The poet has not praised conscience and the cardinal virtues throughout his poem only to abandon them here in favor of need. Also, Need's advice to "bydde and be nedy" conflicts with the frequent attacks in the poem on "bidding and begging." [7] Finally, Need's argument that Christ was "wilfullich nedy" is suspect. It was a favorite argument of the friars, by which they asserted their superiority to the endowed clergy and the monastic orders. By it, also, they defended their theoretical poverty, which was under attack in this period. In his hatred of the friars, the poet would not be likely to subscribe to one of their most successful lines of propaganda.

In attacking need, however, the poet is not denying his own doctrine of patient poverty. The two are quite distinct. Need is primarily the lack of food, drink, and clothing. Though it may involve poverty, it is not the same as the life of patient poverty. They are antithetical in an important respect. Need results in concentration on the provision of bodily needs to the point where they take precedence over the laws

5. xx.1–49.
6. Cf. *Summa Theologica*, II–II, q. 32, vii, ad 3.
7. Cf. xv.219–21, 250–1, and xx.237–8.

of property and morality. Patient poverty, however, leads to a fine disregard for the body's needs (*ne solliciti sitis*), trust in God, and obedience to the law of love. Need's speech is really a warning against the life of need. Need puts man outside the laws of property and morality, outside the guidance of conscience and the cardinal virtues. It makes man lawless. As Need himself says, "Nede ne hath no lawe. . . ." [8] Necessitas non habet legem." [9]

The warning against need in the speech is a warning against friars. For need, if it is not identical with the theoretical poverty of the friars, is the condition resulting from their poverty, and Need's philosophy is the philosophy of "the poor friars." Behind Need's sermon lurk the sophistical friars, cajoling audiences into believing that the friars are most like Christ and that only they are truly holy, for unlike priests and monks and other men, they possess no property and are always needy.[1] A later scene removes any doubt of this relationship between need and the friars, for here the poet states explicitly that the friars are dangerous because of their need. When the friars offer to help Conscience resist the second attack of Antichrist, the character Need reappears and explains why they offered to help. They are motivated by need. He does not use the term. He says they are poor. But the term "need" is supplied in the name of the personification. The friars' poverty or need is their theoretical poverty, the fact that the necessities of life are not provided them by some regular endowment as they are the secular clergy and monks. Need says the friars "come for coueityse to have cure of soules. . . ." They are poor "for patrimoigne hem failleth. . . ." After Need has finished, Conscience says to the friars, If you learn to love, "I wil be ȝowre borghe · ȝe shal haue bred and clothes, And other necessaries i-nowe · ȝow shal no thyng faille. . . ." [2] This scene states clearly what the fallacious doctrine preached by Need in the interlude has already suggested, that their theoretical poverty makes the friars dangerous. Here Need says their need makes them flatter folk; it makes them beg, and beggars lie. It is their need, their theoretical poverty, that Conscience attacks in the conclusion.

This discussion of need and the friars is a reflection of a controversy that flared up again and again in the fourteenth century and later. It is the controversy over the poverty of Christ and the theoretical poverty of the friars, which was based on the claim that Christ Himself was

8. xx.10.
9. *Pupilla oculi*, p. xxxiiᵛ.
1. Cf. the Summoner's account of the friar's preaching, *Canterbury Tales*, D, 1717–23, 1870–1937.
2. xx.228–48.

poor. It was "a well-worn theme" in 1356 [3] when Richard Fitzralph, Archbishop of Armagh, coming to London from Ireland, "fonde þere wise doctors stryue vppon þe beggerie, & beggyng of þe Lord oure Saueoure. & ofte ich was preyed to preche to þe peple, and ich preched seuen sermouns oþer eiȝte to þe peple in her owne tonge." [4] Fitzralph became embroiled in the controversy; and though a papal commission ruled against him, and he died in 1360,[5] neither the controversy nor his part in it was forgotten. Wyclif, [6] Uthred of Boldon,[7] Master Robert Rypon of Durham,[8] and others argued against the friars' doctrine of the poverty of Christ. A chronicling of the controversy is not to the point here. It is enough to show that the argument was current in the poet's time. Involved in it also was the issue of the friars' right to hear confessions. The poet's attack on need and the friars, and on the friars' hearing of confessions, was part of an important intellectual debate, not a manifestation of mere personal hatred.

Both the issue itself and the flavor of the controversy are communicated in Fitzralph's sermon before the pope, *Defensio Curatorum,* translated by Trevisa.[9] Fitzralph argued before the pope the same nine conclusions he had presented in his English sermons in London:

> [1] . . . Oure Lord Ihesus, in his conuersacioun of manhed, alwey was pore, nouȝt for he wolde & loued pouert by-cause of hit-silf. [2] . . . Oure Lord Ihesus neuer beggide wilfulliche. [3] . . . Crist neuer tauȝt wilfulliche to begge. [4] . . . Oure Lord

3. Herbert B. Workman, *John Wyclif, A Study of the English Medieval Church* (Oxford, 1926), *1,* 128. There is a valuable summary of the background of the controversy in Arnold Williams, "Chaucer and the Friars," *Speculum, 28* (1953), 499–513, esp. 500–2.

4. *Defensio,* p. 39.

5. Workman, *1,* 128–30. There are accounts of the controversy in Gwynn, *Studies, 26,* 50–67, and the same writer's *The English Austin Friars in the Time of Wyclif* (Oxford, 1940), pp. 85 ff.; Arnold Williams, 503–4; Pantin, *The English Church,* pp. 151–64; and Dom David Knowles, *The Religious Orders in England* (Cambridge, England, 1955), *2,* 92–3, 95–7.

6. Workman, *2,* 102, 104, and see his references. For a few references in the Wycliffite literature see *The English Works of Wyclif Hitherto Unprinted,* ed. F. D. Matthew, EETS, o.s. *74* (London, 1880), 278, 300.

7. Workman, *1,* 224; Marcett, *Uthred de Boldon,* pp. 8–9; W. A. Pantin, "Two Treatises of Uthred of Boldon on the Monastic Life," in *Studies in Medieval History presented to Frederick Maurice Powicke* (Oxford, 1948), pp. 363–85; Pantin, *The English Church,* pp. 166–75; and Knowles, *Religious Orders in England, 2,* 48–54.

8. G. R. Owst, *Literature and Pulpit in Medieval England* (Cambridge, England, 1933), p. 61, n. 2.

9. For the Latin sermon see Brown, *Fasciculus Rerum Expetendarum & Fugiendarum, 2,* 466–86. Fitzralph's *De Pauperie Salvatoris* is also a document in the controversy. The first four books and the table of contents of the last three are printed in an appendix to John Wyclif, *De Dominio Divino Libri Tres,* ed. Reginald Lane Poole, The Wyclif Society, London, 1890. Bk. VI, "De gradibus paupertatis," pp. 266–70, is particularly relevant.

Ihesus tauȝte þat no man schuld wilfulliche begge. [5] . . . no man may redilich & holiliche wilful beggyng vppon hym take, euermore to holde. [6] . . . hit is nouȝt of þe reule of frere menours, wilful begginge to kepe & holde. [7] . . . þe ferþe pope Alisaundre's bille, þat dampneþ þe libel of maistres, wiþseiþ noon of þe forseide conclusiouns. [8] . . . for parischons of eny chirch to schryue hem wiþ exclusioun of oþer places, þe parische chirche is more worþi to be chosen þan oratory oþer chirche of freres. [9] . . . for parischons of eny chirche to schryue hem onlich to oon persone, þe ordenarye persone is more worþi to be chosen þan eny freres persone.[1]

These "conclusions" parallel at several points the attack on the friars in the last vision of *Dobest*. Fitzralph's detailed argument that Christ "neuer beggide wilfullich"[2] imparts a hollow ring to Need's sermon in the interlude. The praise of need and of begging there is undermined by the Scriptural passages Fitzralph cited to prove that need and begging were against God's law: "In al wise a nedy man & begger schal nouȝt be among ȝow."[3] "Sone be þou nouȝt nedy in þi lif tyme; hit is better be ded þan nedy."[4] "For defaute & for nede many men haueþ y-do amys."[5] "Paul þe apostle dampneþ her trowyng & her opinioun þat trowiþ þat beggerie & gaderyng is holy myldnesse."[6] Such quotations as these, which probably became commonplaces in the course of the dispute, no doubt confirmed the poet in his stand against the friars and their need.[7]

The poet does not only condemn this situation. He suggests, rather tentatively, a solution. If need makes the friars dangerous, if need leads them to transform the sacrament of penance into a meaningless mockery, then the need must be removed. Conscience in his speech to the friars wishes to be rid of it.[8] And in the conclusion Conscience resolves to secure a "fyndyng"[9] for the friars, i.e. "keep, maintenance, provisions, support."[1a] The principle of theoretical poverty which has

1. *Defensio,* pp. 39–40.

2. Ibid., pp. 80–7.

3. Ibid., p. 81. Fitzralph gives Deuteronomy xix as his reference, but apparently it is Deuteronomy xv:4. Cf. the use of the same quotation in *English Works of Wyclif,* Matthew, p. 387.

4. *Defensio,* p. 91 (Ecclesiasticus xl:28 ff.).

5. Ibid., p. 92 (Ecclesiasticus xxvii).

6. Ibid., p. 83 (I Timothy vi).

7. Similar quotations against poverty, biblical in origin but taken from Pope Innocent's *De Contemptu Mundi,* appear in the Man of Law's Prologue, "The Canterbury Tales," B, 113–18, and see Robinson's notes, *Complete Chaucer,* pp. 794–5. Cf. also n. 3, above.

8. xx.241–9.

9. xx.381.

1a. *OED,* "finding," sb., 4. b; see also "find," v., 19. Notice Fitzralph's comment, above, p. 110, n. 6.

let loose a flood of begging, flattering friars on the land must be abandoned. Some regular provision of necessities must be made. The exact nature of the "fyndyng" and the manner of its institution are not specified. But the situation would seem to demand some kind of administrative action within the Church, action by "Piers." It is a clear though muted cry for reform.

A "fyndyng" for the friars establishes a certain limit for interpretation of the more obscure elements in the conclusion, the allusion to Piers the Plowman and the hope that Pride may be destroyed. The poet wants some kind of reform of an institution in this world, the friars. This is undebatable. And this being so, the conclusion can hardly contain at the same time some vision of Judgment Day or a farewell to this world and a hail to the next.

Piers, in this context, cannot be the Christ of the Second Coming, as suggested by H. H. Glunz.[2] Konrad Burdach's interpretation fits the context more satisfactorily. Burdach says the Piers whom Conscience seeks as the poem ends is not Christ but an ideal pope, the executor of the divine will on earth through the power of penance conferred on him by Christ.[3] Nothing more than an ideal pope is needed to reform the friars by giving them a "fyndyng." There is, however, no need to insist that Piers means a good pope here. He can be a good man, or that goodness, that semidivine quality in human nature which, as Burdach argues so effectively, lies behind the conception of Piers. The poet can be expressing the hope that mankind has the capacity to reform the friars and open the way to salvation. The context does not allow one to go beyond this view of a *human* Piers.

Similarly limited is Conscience's hope that Piers will destroy Pride. Though it may seem like a plea for a perfect age such as only Christ could bring, the context bars the way. A recurrent vision of a day of universal peace and love and of a sinless generation does pervade the poem, but it is based on the poet's belief in the goodness of man and on contemporary hopes for such an era,[4] rather than on a vision of the Second Coming. Actually, the first vision of *Dobest* has shown how pride can be destroyed. There, when Pride attacked Christendom, Conscience told mankind they were not strong enough to oppose pride unless grace was with them. But the implication is clear that when in a state of grace, mankind can resist and destroy pride. In the scene, mankind repents sincerely, and Conscience rejoices: I care nought, he cries, though Pride comes now.[5] Obviously mankind can conquer and

---

2. *Literarästhetik*, pp. 533, 534–5.
3. *Ackermann*, p. 314.
4. As, for instance, in John de Pera-Tallada's *Vade mecum in tribulatione*, Brown, *Fasciculus Rerum Expetendarum*, 2, 496–508.
5. XIX.352–80.

"destroy" pride when restored to grace by true repentance. Conscience's call in the conclusion for the destruction of pride need mean little more than this. If the friars are reformed and true penance is possible, man can destroy pride, i.e. successfully wage war against mortal sin.

This explanation of the last vision and its conclusion does not reduce it to triviality or anticlimax. True, the conclusion envisions nothing so grandiose as the Second Coming. Nevertheless, the issue is one of tremendous import. The salvation of mankind is still the theme. In *Dobest* the poet has portrayed the gifts of the Third Person of the Trinity which complete the scheme of salvation and has shown man using and abusing those gifts. He has warned his generation, furthermore, of two dangers which disrupt the scheme and imperil men's souls. Both are bound up with the system of penance by which weak and sinful man is restored to grace so that he may be saved. One danger is within man: it is his reluctance to pay *redde quod debes,* to restore what he has wrongfully taken from his fellow men, to forgive others their injuries to him, to obey the law of love and the cardinal virtues. The other danger is outside man: it is the friars' corruption of the sacrament of penance so that men are not truly contrite and are not restored to grace.

The poet's artistic vision is moralistic rather than raptly prophetic, realistic rather than mystical. The poem closes with both a warning and a note of hope.[6] There is neither universal darkness nor the supernal vision. The climactic battle with the sins and Antichrist has produced splendid Beethovian thunder, but the final chords are muted and unresolved. This is neither a tragedy nor a comedy, for the drama of salvation continues as long as mankind exists and as long as there is a Piers Plowman, a goodness and a divinity in man. There is nothing trivial, however, in this conclusion in which nothing is concluded. Conscience's cry for grace which closes the poem is nothing less than a cry for and a faith in the salvation of man. And the salvation of man is the great theme of the whole poem. It is the poem's reason for being.

6. Burdach comments that the final vision "trembles in fear and hope for the future of mankind" (*Ackermann,* p. 314). I have reviewed some of the varying comments on the mood of the poem at its close in "The Conclusion of *Piers Plowman," JEGP, 49* (1950), 309. The discussion of Sister Rosa Bernard Donna, *Despair and Hope, A Study in Langland and Augustine* (Washington, D.C., 1948), pp. 65-73, 176-82, pertains to theological hope and despair, not the poet's mood. See E. Talbot Donaldson's review in *MLN, 68* (1953), 141-2.

Bibliographical Index

THIS is chiefly an index to authors or works quoted, discussed, or cited in the text or notes. Titles of books and subjects of articles are listed after the names of their authors or editors, and page references are given for the individual works. Anonymous works are entered under both title and editor. Full bibliographical data for each work are given in the Cue Titles or on the first page referred to.